The Power of Principles

The Power of Principles

ETHICS FOR THE NEW CORPORATE CULTURE

WILLIAM J. BYRON, S.J.

ORBIS BOOKS

Maryknoll, New York 10545

Founded in 1970, Orbis Books endeavors to publish works that enlighten the mind, nourish the spirit, and challenge the conscience. The publishing arm of the Maryknoll Fathers and Brothers, Orbis seeks to explore the global dimensions of the Christian faith and mission, to invite dialogue with diverse cultures and religious traditions, and to serve the cause of reconciliation and peace. The books published reflect the views of their authors and do not represent the official position of the Maryknoll Society. To learn more about Maryknoll and Orbis Books, please visit our website at www.maryknoll.org.

Library of Congress Cataloging-in-Publication Data

Byron, William J., 1927-
    The power of principles : ethics for the new corporate culture / William J. Byron.
        p. cm.
    Includes bibliographical references and index.
    ISBN-13: 978-1-57075-678-8 (pbk.)
    1. Business ethics. 2. Corporate culture. 3. Social responsibility of business. I. Title.
    HF5387.B97 2006
    174'.4—dc22
                                                2006009454

For
Gerry Roche,
good friend, great executive recruiter.

CONTENTS

The Power of Principles

"Merrill Lynch" is a name as familiar as "Wall Street" in financial and business circles. Well before the collapse of Enron and the surge of outrage over corruption in corporate America, a print advertisement highlighting Merrill Lynch's self-proclaimed "commitment to a set of principles," formulated in 1993 as applicable to the changing world of business, appeared in many major newspapers. Merrill Lynch, to its embarrassment, did not pass unscathed through the ethical scandals that rocked American business several years later. You may recall, for example, that the Securities and Exchange Commission found four former Merrill Lynch executives, including the chairman of its investment banking division, guilty of aiding and abetting securities fraud at one of the firm's famous clients, none other than Enron. In an editorial titled "Sweeping Up the Street," *Business Week* said, "We now know that the half-truths and full lies of analysts such as Merrill Lynch & Co.'s Henry Blodgett . . . did not go unnoticed within their firms. . . . [A]larms did, in fact, go off on the Street—but managers chose to ignore them."[1]

The point of this introductory observation is not to denounce Merrill Lynch, but to highlight the fact that principles can guide business decision makers who open their minds to ethical guidance—and to add the point that those principles can also be ignored.

Before discussing my set of "old ethical principles," first I would like to consider the Merrill Lynch principles. They are:

(1) client focus; (2) respect for the individual; (3) teamwork; (4) responsible citizenship; and (5) integrity. There is nothing particularly new about any of these, and although "client focus" is not necessarily an ethical principle, the other four clearly are.

"Respect for the individual" is another way of stating the classic *principle of the dignity of the human person*. This is a bedrock principle of both personal and social ethics.

"Teamwork" is another way of stating the ethical *principle of participation*, or *principle of association,* which rests on the *principle of human dignity* and assures that the human person, precisely because of his or her inherent dignity as a person, has a right to a voice in workplace decision making, as well as a right to associate with others in the workplace, and, as an employee, he or she has the right to organize with other employees for the protection and advancement of employee rights. It is the right, in brief, not to be silenced and excluded.

Merrill Lynch's principle of "responsible citizenship" is another way of saying "corporate social responsibility," which means that a firm acknowledges an obligation to be *responsive* to community needs and *responsible* for the advancement of the common good. It is the obligation to promote and protect genuine community interests. The corporate social responsibility model, as elaborated in business school textbooks,[2] builds first on the foundation of economic viability and profitability, which simply means that a fundamental economic level of responsibility (measured in profitably) must be met if the enterprise is to remain in existence. The corporate social responsibility model then moves up to the legal level, where the responsible corporation does everything the law requires it to do (e.g., product safety, fair employment practices, truth in advertising). Next comes the ethical level, where the socially responsible corporation recognizes that there are things it *should* do, that it is ethically obligated to do, that are not legally prescribed. Finally, there is a fourth level of corporate social responsibility called "discretionary" or "philanthropic responsibility," where the corporation goes beyond not only what is legally required, but also what it judges as a strictly ethical obligation. At this level the corporation does what is "good" for the community, not because economic, legal, or ethical considerations require it, but simply because it is good to do. At this level, religious motivation may "oblige" a person to act, even though ethical arguments derived from reason, not revelation, would not so urge. In other words, a person's religious convictions might drive him or her beyond what purely rational, ethical reflection would require. I am impressed by how common it is for men and women who are committed to the Jewish faith to consider themselves clearly obliged, as Jews, to be philanthropic and attentive to community needs. The distinction between ethical action understood as behavior based on reason, and "doing the right thing" because revelation and religious faith require it, is not all that evident. Most ethical acts are clearly rooted in both reason and revelation.

The socially responsible corporation operates on all four levels, and there is nothing particularly new about this. There have been in the past and continue to be in the present some good, responsible corporate citizens in the American economy. However, there have also been plenty of corporate renegades; and, as everyone is now painfully aware, new rogue executives and relatively new corporate names are facing disgrace and criminal penalties.

"Integrity" is Merrill Lynch's fifth principle. This one word really says it all in any discussion of ethics, and it will have a prominent place in the pages of *The Power of Principles*. There is certainly nothing new about the principle of integrity, unless you want to argue that many organizations might "try it again for the first time," or that in some corporations the principle of integrity "is just like new" because it has never been used.

My intention in presenting these principles here at the outset is not to sing the praises of Merrill Lynch, where there could at any time be a shortfall between the level of proclaimed principle and the record of performance. Rather, the reference to a real organization in the real world of work helps to keep what I propose to offer in this book, namely down-to-earth advice on "the Street" (i.e., Wall Street).

So permit me to quote some more of Merrill Lynch's ad copy: "These principles are the beliefs that define the way we conduct our business." That, of course, is exactly as it should be. "It is our commitment to them that guides every one of our actions and is at the heart of all the advice we provide—in 35 countries around the world." Not all companies would be so confident about their ability to apply uniform ethical standards to their behavior at home and abroad, where different cultures may condone, and perhaps even require, some variations in behavior. The Foreign Corrupt Practices Act was enacted by the U.S. Congress in 1977 and signed into law to permit U.S. firms to remain competitive overseas by allowing business practices there (within a well-defined limit) that would be legally impermissible here. A case in point is the distinction between a bribe, always prohibited by both law and ethics here and abroad, and a "grease payment," forbidden here, but expected as part of the normal way of doing business in some countries just to speed up a process, for example, for a permit or a service that a public official should provide but will not, unless an incentive of extra payment is given. This is quite different from paying or bribing someone *not* to do what his or her job requires, or to do something that he or she should never do.

The Merrill Lynch advertisement goes on to say, "Our reputation as a company that lives by its principles is important to us. . . . We do not judge ourselves solely by the numbers, but how we live up to our principles."

This is a good norm for anyone, in any organization, at any time. Judge yourself not just by the numbers, but by how you live up to your principles. It's a shame that Merrill Lynch did not live up to this norm.

Principles, I want to stress, are initiating impulses; they are internalized convictions that produce action. Principles direct your actions and your choices. Your principles help to define who you are. Principles are beginnings; they lead to something. That's why I like to say, "On the road to success in business, you should let your principles do the driving."

The "principles" (with the "le" at the end of the word instead of the "al") that business professors encourage college students to comprehend in the classroom have the potential to l-e-a-d them through the thicket of a problem to be solved, or a decision to be made, on their way to the future. *Principles lead to something.* The corporate world needs principled leaders and followers to lift corporate life to a higher plane than the one business people, in general, are walking as they move into the twenty-first century. This need to elevate corporate life underscores the not-so-modest goal of this book, namely, an exposition of the principles, that, if internalized, will provide direction and prompt behavior in business decision makers to enable them to steer clear of the ethical quicksand that sunk Enron, Arthur Andersen, and others in the beginning of this century.

Definitions of the word "principle" from dictionaries or textbooks will not provide direction or prompt behavior. Descriptions and examples from the experience of principled persons who have been in the trenches for awhile, if delivered in clear expository prose, will, and that is what I attempt in this book.

It is worth noting that a virtue also leads to something good. A virtue is a power, a force for good. All virtues are values, but, as a moment's reflection will attest, not all values are virtues. For example, wealth is a dominant value in the lives of some people, and it can lead to greed if it directs all they think about and do. Similarly, fame, pleasure (we have all heard of the "pleasure principle"), and jealousy are dominant values in many lives; you wouldn't identify these as virtues. It is always important to know what drives you and whether your values are taking you in the right direction.

Again, "let your principles do the driving" if you want to remain on the high road en route to success in business.

I am convinced that what I will be identifying as "old" ethical principles in the pages that follow have direct relevance to the business world that young men and women are now entering. Those who know their way around in that world will be heard from in subsequent chapters. The final chapter in the book—"From One Generation to Another"—conveys some direct messages from veterans to newcomers and those not yet fixed in their ways of doing business. One such veteran—George M. Ferris, Jr., of the financial services company Ferris, Baker, Watts—passed along a favorite quotation from Mahatma Gandhi; he thought it should be shared with the young and I agree. I offer it now, simply to call attention to the phrase "without principle" at the end. According to Ferris, who is a 1950 graduate of Harvard Business School, Gandhi said that there are "seven sins in the world: wealth without work, pleasure without conscience, knowledge without character, commerce without morality, science without humanity, worship without sacrifice, and politics without principle."

This book hopes to call attention to work, conscience, character, morality, humanity, sacrifice, and principle. It is not an exposé in the wake of Enron, WorldCom, Adelphi and the other ethical scandals that have blackened the eye of business in America in recent years. It is an exercise in expository prose intended to engage the minds and consciences of those who are now, or hope soon to be, decision makers in the American business system. "If we always had to think about ethics around here, we'd never get anything done," says the severe-looking boss to a harried underling in a famous Bo Brown cartoon. I am hopeful that readers of this book will become convinced that if they always think about ethics on the job, they will get a lot more done more efficiently and more profitably than they might now suspect.

Let us now move to a brief synopsis of the Enron situation because I view Enron, and everything their name now implies, as the context for the reflection and conversation that this book is intended to stimulate.

Representative James C. Greenwood, a Republican of Pennsylvania, was chairman of the investigative subcommittee of the House Energy and Commerce Committee when it decided to investigate the Enron situation. At a January 24, 2002, hearing, Greenwood said to David B. Duncan, the dismissed Arthur Andersen partner who was accused of orchestrating the destruction of documents in the Enron case, "Mr. Duncan, Enron robbed the bank. Arthur Andersen provided the getaway car, and they say you were at the wheel." Mr. Duncan, on advice from his lawyers, asserted his constitutional right under the Fifth Amendment and declined to reply.

It is easy to substitute blame for analysis. There is more than enough blame to go around for the Enron collapse. Analysis is harder to come by. Analytical comments now will be useful as a way to examine principled behavior, or its absence, in American business.

In the wake of the bankruptcy, one Enron executive committed suicide, others resigned, thousands of employees lost their jobs, and even more were left holding empty 401(k) bags. Greed, deceit, mismanagement, and multiple conflicts of interest figured in all of this, as did the purchase of political influence in the soft-money swamp that will never be drained unless Congress imposes on itself serious and binding campaign finance reform. This case also involves accounting fraud, insider trading, and illegal destruction of documents.

It is not enough to call the Enron collapse a "systemic" failure. Systems are made up of decision-making persons. In the Enron-Andersen debacle, human beings chose to act unethically.

Enron started out as a natural-gas pipeline company. In an environment of deregulation, Enron became an unregulated, energy contract-trading company with relatively few real assets. If you are a trading company, all you really have is your credit. Enron lost both credit and credibility. It tried to hide its losses by inflating earnings reports and shifting debt from its balance sheet to newly created off-balance-sheet partnerships. For the "system" to work, the public has to be able to trust the numbers. This means trusting those who post the numbers (management) and those who certify them to be in conformity with generally accepted accounting standards (outside auditors).

The company failed to warn its employees of impending doom. In fact, it positively misled employees to believe the company was strong and prevented employees from selling the Enron stock in their 401(k) retirement plans (because the company switched plan administrators, thus putting a freeze on transactions) at the same time top executives of the company were unloading theirs.

Congress failed, under heavy industry lobbying, to pass laws that would prevent Enron from doing risky trading online that extended far beyond energy transactions. In fact, in 1992 Congress exempted Enron and other power marketers from oversight by the Commodity Futures Trading Commission. Congress also failed to respond to a plea from then chairman of the Securities and Exchange Commission, Arthur Levitt, Jr., to impose tough conflict-of-interest restrictions on accounting firms. Had Congress been able to resist pressure from lobbyists for the big accounting firms, it would have been illegal for Arthur Andersen, Enron's outside auditor, to be a paid consultant to the company that it was also engaged to audit. In the year before the collapse, Andersen reportedly received $27 million from Enron in consulting fees while earning $25 million as Enron's auditor.

Another fault, shared by the company and the Congress, is the failure to regulate the amount of Enron stock that employees held in their retirement accounts. It is foolish to have all your retirement assets in the stock of one company. By overloading their employees' defined contribution retirement plans with Enron stock (and encouraging the employees to buy more Enron stock themselves), the company shifted the risk involved in the retirement plan to the employee. (There is a lesson to be learned here by those who think that individual

Social Security retirement accounts should be privatized.)

Ethics means doing the right thing. However, Enron took an end run around ethics, and Andersen certified the company's questionable playbook.

Bethany McLean and Peter Elkind, senior staff writers for *Fortune* magazine, tell the Enron story in their book, *The Smartest Guys in the Room: The Amazing Rise and Scandalous Fall of Enron.*[3] This should be required reading for anyone interested in gaining an appreciation of the context within which the conversation about the need for principled ethical behavior in American business is taking place. In the Introduction to their book, McLean and Elkind write:

> In the public eye, Enron's mission was nothing more than the cover story for a massive fraud. But what brought Enron down was something more complex—and more tragic—than simple thievery. The tale of Enron is a story of human weakness, of hubris and greed and rampant self-delusion; of ambition run amok; of a grand experiment in the deregulated world; of a business model that didn't work; and of smart people who believed their next gamble would cover their last disaster—and who couldn't admit they were wrong.[4]

Principled behavior on the part of all the principals would have, quite literally, made all the difference in the world for Enron and the American business system. As summarized in *The Economist* in 2003, "the main dangers to the success of capitalism are the very people who would consider themselves its most ardent advocates: the bosses of companies, the owners of companies, and the politicians who tirelessly insist that they are 'pro-business.' At the intersection of these groups lies most of what is wrong with capitalism, and the best opportunities to make that system even more successful than it has been thus far."[5] The editors give some words of advice to political and economic decision makers in the American system:

Many of the corporate scandals that America, especially, has endured in recent years reflect outright criminality. A lawful order knows what to do with criminals, and pro-business politicians are in truth militantly anti-capitalist if they flinch from cracking down on bosses' crimes. The other great ongoing scandal is not a matter of law-breaking: it is that bosses have grown accustomed to rewarding themselves like owners, though bearing few risks of ownership—while the real owners, shareholders in the companies concerned, have let them get on with it. Pro-business politicians who regard this vacuum of accountable control as a private matter of no wider concern are doing capitalism a grave disservice. A system that gives a charter to brazen unchecked greed is a system in peril.[6]

I have no quarrel with the editors' assessment of both greed and peril in this present situation. I would be slow, however, to acknowledge that all stockholders are true "owners" in the classic meaning of the term. Many of them are just speculators whose "investment" in a company is shallow, even though their holdings may be extensive, and their ownership is sufficiently transitory that they will sell at the drop of a hat, not to mention a fall in share price. Nonetheless, the point about a "vacuum of accountable control" is well taken; attention must be paid—and paid soon.

I offer this book as a modest contribution to the challenge of filling the vacuum of accountable control. I will repeat myself and say that "principled behavior on the part of the principals" would have prevented the collapse of Enron, Arthur Andersen, and others; the purpose of *The Power of Principles* is simply to outline the principles that I hope the next generation of principals will internalize and have both the good sense and the quiet courage to follow.

The Power of Principles

CHAPTER ONE

Old Ethical Principles

For a simple, down-to-earth, practical illustration of articulating a dominant value, translating that value into a principle, and allowing that principle to influence a culture, I would refer the reader to a summer camp in Westport, in upstate New York, on the shore of Lake Champlain. Camp Dudley has been there since 1885. Founded by the YMCA, it is now an independent corporation, governed by a board of trustees, and operates as a nondenominational Christian camp for boys, ages seven to fifteen, under a motto that expresses the dominant value and thus defines the culture of this camp. That motto is: "The Other Fellow First."

I spend a long weekend at Dudley every summer as a guest chaplain—one of a number of guest clergy, male and female, of different denominations—to lead a noon Sunday interfaith chapel service in an outdoor "chapel" of long-log "benches" on a tree-lined slope running down to a bluff that overlooks the lake. There is a platform there equipped with lectern, microphone, organ, and chairs for readers, cantors, and the leader of prayer who is also the "chapel speaker."

Some years ago my visit to Dudley coincided with Parents' Weekend. Soon after arriving on Friday afternoon, I happened to meet a couple from New York City who had come to visit their eight-year-old son. He was experiencing his first extended absence from home. His parents mentioned that their boy had been having a few adjustment problems in his Upper East Side private elementary school, and they were anxious to see how he was getting along at camp. A few minutes later the youngster, a bit overweight, came waddling up to greet his parents. He was introduced to me, and just to make a bit of ice-breaking conversation, I asked, "What do you like best about Camp Dudley?" His immediate response: "Nobody here makes fun of you."

That response says a lot about culture-shaping behavior. It also suggests the wisdom of encapsulating the organization's central value in a motto ("The Other Fellow First") that conveys the organization's culture.

PRINCIPLES AND CULTURE

Principles are internalized values and values define cultures. Before providing a general overview of "old" ethical principles, I want to say a few words about culture.

A culture is a set of shared meanings, principles, and values.[1] Values, as I indicated, define cultures. Where values are widely shared, and the sharing bonds together with common ties those who hold the same values, you have an identifiable culture. There are as many different cultures as there are distinct sets of shared meanings, principles, and values. This is not to say that everyone in a given culture is the same. No, you have diversity of age, wealth, class, intelligence, education, and responsibility in a given culture where diverse people are unified by a shared belief system, a set of agreed-upon principles, a collection of common values. They literally have a lot in common and thus differ from other people in other settings who hold a lot of other things in common. You notice it in law firms, hospitals, colleges, corporations—wherever people comment on the special "culture" that characterizes the place.

In a tribute to Nebraska, written in 1923 upon completion of her novel *A Lost Lady*, Willa Cather said:

We must face the fact that the splendid story of the pioneers is finished, and that no new story worthy to take its place has yet begun. . . . The generation now in the driver's seat hates to make anything, wants to live and die in an automobile, scudding past those acres where the old men used to follow the corn-rows up and down. They want to buy everything ready-made: clothes, food, education, music, pleasure. Will the third generation—the full-blooded joyous ones just coming over the hill—be fooled? Will it believe that to live easily is to live happily?[2]

Subsequent generations have been fooled. Perhaps each generation has to learn for itself, but the experience of previous generations, as I hope to demonstrate in the final chapter of this book, can help the young identify and understand the values that will eventually constitute the sets of shared meanings in new, and one might hope, better cultures.

Jesuit prep schools today say they are educating "men and women for others." The U.S. Army invites you to "be all that you can be." Hewlett-Packard wants to do things "the H-P way." "Cornellcares.com" is one medical center's Web address offering innovative tools, strategies, and advice related to geriatric mental health. The Web address expresses a value wrapped in a slogan: "Cornell cares." And so it goes throughout the world of slogan communication here on earth and out in cyberspace.

The old corporate culture in America was characterized by values like freedom, individualism, competition, loyalty, thrift, stability, fidelity to contract, efficiency, self-reliance, power, and profit. If not controlled (regulated) by self, or by social norms, or by public law, pursuit of some of these values could be fueled by unworthy values like greed and the desire to dominate (rather than a desire to serve) and thus propel a person or a firm into unethical territory.

The new (or newer, or most recent) corporate culture is defined by many, but not all, of these same values, although they are interpreted now somewhat differently. And there are some new values emerging in the new corporate context, as will be explained more fully in the next chapter.

Whereas the old (say, 50 years ago) corporate culture would

tolerate an employer's not looking much beyond the interests of a firm's shareholders, the new corporate culture has grown comfortable with the notion of "stakeholder" and sees an ethical connection between the firm and not only its shareholders, but all others who have a stake in what that firm does: employees, suppliers, customers, the broader community, and the physical environment, to name just a few. The outlook is more communitarian, more attentive to the dictates of the common good. There was some of this in the past, a "social compact" between employer and employee that was somewhat paternalistic and relatively free of both the deregulation and foreign competition that have caused much of the present economic dislocation in America. However, the dominant value of the old corporate culture was individualism, not regard for the other, and certainly not "communitarianism"— an ideology both explained and praised by George Lodge to classes of not-readily-receptive business executives in the Advanced Management Program at the Harvard Business School in the 1970s (and later published in *The New American Ideology*).[3] There is a good deal of evidence now that individualism is again on the rise. Greed's ugly head has risen high above the surface once again in corporate America. There are also some encouraging signs that communitarian concerns are influencing the decisions of some major corporations that want to balance corporate self-interest with community concerns.

Note, for example, what William Clay Ford, Jr., chairman of Ford Motor Company, told Jeffrey Garten in an undated interview for Garten's 2001 book *The Mind of the C.E.O.*: "At the end of the [twentieth] century, many of the great ideological issues are off the table. It's now a question of what consumers are going to be demanding, rather than what business leaders are envisioning. Consumers want a safer, cleaner, more equitable world, and they'll buy from companies that display those characteristics. I believe that companies that are responsive to those needs—assuming they have great products and services, of course—will have a commanding market position."[4]

Ford had his words thrown back at him in a full-page "open

letter" advertisement that ran in the *New York Times* on December 2, 2004, under the heading "Gas Guzzling Is Un-American." Signed by Michael Brune, Executive Director, Rainforest Action Network, the letter read in part:

> When you took the helm, you announced Ford Motor Company's "Cleaner, Safer, Sooner" campaign and raised our hopes that a self-avowed "life-long environmentalist" was now running America's flagship automaker. We believed you then, but four years later the facts tell a very different story. Ford has ranked dead last among all major automakers in overall fuel efficiency every year since you became CEO. Since the oil crisis of the 1970s, the EPA has ranked your company last in overall fuel efficiency for 20 out of the last 30 years. Ford's fleet today gets fewer miles per gallon on average than the Model-T did 80 years ago.

The letter ends on this accusatory note: "In October 2000 you said that your vision was 'to achieve new levels of success as a business, and clear leadership in resolving social and environmental issues.' Mr. Ford, if this is your best, then your best won't do. America deserves better."

It would have been just about inconceivable in 1950 to imagine airplanes, office buildings, restaurants, and college residence halls that are all smoke-free. In the same way no one then gave a thought to picking up after their dogs in the interest of neighborhood aesthetics, not to mention sanitation. Increased sensitivity over environmental and health concerns is just one small piece of evidence of a value shift away from mindless individualism toward a more enlightened communitarian outlook.

THE OLD ETHICAL PRINCIPLES

In any case, here, in brief outline, are what I call "old ethical principles" that can, I believe, surface in individual and community consciousness to meet the ethical challenges of our new corporate culture. Defining elements of this new culture, as well as a fuller exposition of each of the old ethical principles, will be spelled out in subsequent chapters. Meanwhile, bear in mind that although principles can be neglected, they, unlike laws, cannot be broken. They are always there, waiting to be applied, although they can be permitted to lie dormant. Principles have no loopholes.

I've identified ten classic ethical principles and invite the reader to come up with his or her own understanding of each one. You are the world's leading expert on your own opinion. It is important that you articulate your own opinion on these matters so that you can assess how widely shared, in your present or future workplace, are your values and the understandings you have of these classic principles. Remember, a culture is a set of shared meanings and values. How widely shared are your meanings and values relative to these ten points?

First, the Principle of Integrity. I think of integrity in terms of wholeness, solidity of character, honesty, trustworthiness, and responsibility. What would you add or subtract from that list?

Second, the Principle of Veracity. This, to me, involves telling the truth in all circumstances; it also includes accountability and transparency.

Third, the Principle of Fairness. By this, of course, I mean justice, treating equals equally, giving to everyone his or her due.

Fourth, the Principle of Human Dignity. This bedrock principle of all ethics—personal and organizational—acknowledges a person's inherent worth. It prompts respectful recognition of another's value simply for being human.

Fifth, the Principle of Participation, workplace participation in this case. This principle respects another's right not to be ignored on the job or shut out from decision making within the organization.

Sixth, the Principle of Commitment. What I have in mind

here is that a committed person can be counted on for dependability, reliability, fidelity, loyalty.

Seventh, the Principle of Social Responsibility. This points to an obligation to look to the interests of the broader community and to treat the community as a stakeholder in what the corporation or organization does.

Eighth, the Principle of the Common Good. This operates as an antidote to individualism; it aligns one's personal interests with the community's well-being. This may indeed be the most difficult of all these principles around which to form an organizational consensus relating to the common good of the corporation and then relating that understanding to an understanding of the broader common good outside the organization.

Ninth, the Principle of Subsidiarity. This might best be understood in terms of delegation and decentralization, keeping decision making close to the ground. (I'll call it the principle of delegation when I give it fuller treatment in Chapter 11, simply because "subsidiarity" is an unfamiliar term to most American readers.) It means that no decision should be taken at a higher level that can be made as effectively and efficiently at a lower level in the organization. This could be viewed as a "principle of respect for proper autonomy." It could also be understood in terms of Saul Alinsky's "Iron Rule" for his Industrial Areas Foundation: "Never, never do for others what they can do for themselves."

Tenth, the Ethical Principle of Love. I see this as a principle, an internalized conviction, that prompts a willingness to sacrifice one's time, convenience, and a share of one's ideas and material goods for the good of others.

Some of these would coincide with what William Faulkner, in his famous acceptance speech upon receiving the Nobel Prize in Literature, called "the old verities." By these he meant "truths of the heart, the universal truths lacking which any story is ephemeral and doomed." Specifically, he was thinking of "love and honor and pity and pride and compassion and sacrifice."[5] Even those in my set of ten that are not quite so grand are, nonetheless, principles—lofty, but not so far above the fray that they cannot be applied on the ground in business decision making. Their application will, by the way, prove that Oliver Wendell Holmes, Jr., was clever, but not necessarily correct when he remarked in 1897 that "a man is usually more careful of his money than of his principles."

THE CORNER OFFICE

The search for business, organizational, or corporate ethics will lead directly to the corner office, to the executive suite, to the person and character of the CEO. This raises a question I will not explore in depth in this book: Is there a direct connection between the personal morality in the private life of the CEO, and the organizational morality in the public, moral person of a corporation, institution, or organized collection of the many persons, who, working under the leadership of a CEO, try to achieve an organizational purpose? I prescind from the question of whether a man who, for example, is unfaithful to his wife can lead an ethical organization, or whether a woman who habitually lies to a friend can lead her organization to a high and consistent level of ethical integrity. It is easy to judge but hard to measure the correlation between the personal character of the leader and the institutional integrity of the organization. I do not attempt anything along those lines here, but it is a question that I regard as worthy of careful consideration and study, all the more so after the March 2005 forced resignation of the Boeing Company's CEO, Harry C. Stonecipher, who, when confronted by his board, admitted to having a consensual "personal relationship" with a female Boeing executive.

Boeing's code of ethical business conduct, applicable to all employees, makes no mention of sexual misconduct, but states, "Employees must not engage in conduct or activity that may raise questions as to the company's honesty, impartiality, or reputation or otherwise cause embarrassment to the company."[6] Stonecipher, who had come out of retirement 15 months earlier to restore the company's credibility after several widely publicized ethical scandals, did not protest the board's action, saying that it acted "fairly," and that he had "used poor judgment."[7] Part of the poor judgment, according to one observer, was his decision "to detail his actions and desires in a series of very explicit e-mails to the woman in question."[8]

Around the same time, Holland & Knight, the second largest law firm in Florida and the fifteenth largest in the United States, drew embarrassing headlines when the *St. Petersburg Times* disclosed that the firm had promoted Douglas A. Wright, one of its tax lawyers, to chief operating partner in the 1,250-lawyer Tampa office, knowing that an internal investigation had found him guilty a year earlier of sexual harassment. Nine female lawyers in that office had accused him of harassing them. When the story became public, he resigned the new position but retained his partnership.

In a 2003 "Ideas & Trends" essay in the Sunday *New York Times*, Geoffrey Nunberg acknowledges that America "does have a culture of the corporation," but "it is increasingly detached from the values that are touchstones in our personal dealings. Few people nowadays perceive the historical connection between 'private sector' and 'private life.' "[9] The private lives of those who hold executive responsibility in the private sector reflect personal character and probably do—although there are no scientific studies to support this conclusion—influence corporate behavior for good or ill.

Writing in *The Wall Street Journal* on January 23, 2004, Jack Welch, the retired chairman of GE, spoke of the "four essential traits of leadership." He listed them as (1) energy, (2) the ability to energize others, (3) having an edge ("the courage to make tough yes-or-no decisions—no maybes"), and (4) the ability to execute. If a candidate for a leadership role has all four of these, wrote Welch, "then you look for a final trait—passion. By that I mean a heartfelt, deep and authentic excitement about life and work." But, according to Welch, "you cannot even start to think about the Four E's until you get a solid yes on two questions":

First: Does the leadership candidate have integrity? That means, does he or she tell the truth, take responsibility for past actions, admit mistakes and fix them? Does he demonstrate fairness, loyalty, goodness, compassion? Does she listen to others? Does he truly value human dignity and voice? These may seem like fuzzy, subjective questions, but you have to get a strong "AMEN" in your gut to all of them to even consider a person as a leader.

Second: Before applying the Four E's, you have to ask, is the candidate intelligent? That doesn't mean a leader must have read Kant and Shakespeare. . . . It does mean the candidate has to have the breadth of knowledge, from history to science, which allows him to lead other smart people in a world that is getting more complex by the minute. Further, a leader's intelligence has to have a strong emotional component. He has to have high levels of self-awareness, maturity and self-control. She must be able to withstand the heat, handle setbacks and, when those lucky moments arise, enjoy success with equal parts of joy and humility.

In her opening remarks to the jury in the famous Martha Stewart trial of 2004, Assistant U.S. Attorney Karen Patton Seymour said: "Ladies and gentlemen, lying to federal agents, obstructing justice, committing perjury, fabricating evidence and cheating investors in the stock market—these are serious crimes." Indeed they are. And although her organization— Martha Stewart Living Omnimedia, Inc.—was not on trial, the faults and failures of Martha Stewart raised questions about the ethics of the organization she headed, questions the organization seems to have been able to handle to the satisfaction of shareholders and outside observers.

Around that same time, Paul Krugman's February 8, 2004, *New York Times* review of two books "about C.E.O.'s who looted their companies and the financial press that covered up for them," opened with these words:

Eighteen months ago, American capitalism seemed to be in crisis. Stocks had plunged, and some of the nation's most celebrated business leaders had been exposed as phonies if not crooks. Now the economy is growing, and the Dow's been back above 10,000. So is it safe to buy stocks again? After you read Roger Lowenstein's *Origins of the Crash* [*The Great Bubble and Its Undoing*: Penguin Press] and Maggie Mahar's *Bull!* [*A History of the Boom, 1982-1999*: HarperBusiness] you'll have serious doubts. Both tell the story, from different angles, of how ordinary investors got suckered into supporting the lifestyle of the rich and shameless. And you have to wonder whether anything has really changed.

Krugman's review goes on to say: "Lowenstein's title may convey the impression that his book is mainly about stock prices. It isn't: it's about the epidemic of corruption that spread through corporate America in the 1990s, though that epidemic was in part both an effect and a cause of the bull market. A better title might have been 'Executives Gone Wild.' "

Do these executives have integrity? Hardly. Do their organizations embody high levels of ethics? Not likely. Part of the problem in the case of errant CEOs is a lack of oversight on the part of governing boards, and where wrongdoing occurred at lower ranks of executive responsibility, the problem is a failure of higher-ups to monitor what was going on below them.

To engage itself honestly and effectively with the issue of organizational ethics, a board of directors has to first take a good look at itself, as is happening in corporate America in the wake of Sarbanes-Oxley. Some boards are under investigation for questionable business ties between directors and the corporations they serve. The awarding of sweetheart business deals by boards to their members and members' companies, a practice that goes by the name of self-dealing, still goes on with token avoidance of the appearance of impropriety by permitting directors to recuse themselves from votes on matters in which they would benefit financially. To the extent that mixed or self-serving motives bring a director to a seat on a governing board, it is likely that an erosion of ethics will become a problem for the organization.

After describing, in *Origins of the Crash*, the problems that triggered several of the major corporate scandals, Roger Lowenstein writes: "It is fair to wonder why directors went along with such abuses, and the answer has its roots in the distinct culture of America's boardrooms."[10] Elements of that culture are: (1) the twinning of the positions of chairman and CEO in one person ("think how inappropriate would the description President and Chief Justice sound, or Head Coach and Quarterback," Lowenstein says); (2) the "fraternal" character of boardrooms (Lowenstein calls them "modern oases of gentility"); (3) long tenure; (4) interlocking directorships (so that the watchers were also being watched by those they were overseeing); (5) use of compensation consultants whose recommended salary hikes for the CEO would boost the average against which outside directors, who were also CEOs, would have their compensation compared; and (6) an accepted boardroom etiquette where, in Warren Buffet's words, to stand up and criticize the CEO felt like "belching" at the table.[11]

CULTURE AND TRUST

It all comes down to culture and trust. What is the dominant value that defines the culture, not just of the boardroom but of the entire organization? How widely is it shared throughout the organization? How trustworthy are the leaders in an organization? How trustworthy are they perceived to be by those they lead in that organization? How fully encompassing is the trust that generates the energy and purifies the air of the organization that has a claim on the time, talent, and commitment of all who work there? Trust is something of an elusive concept. The enemy of trust is secrecy. What is the substance, the texture, the fabric of a trusting relationship in business? Answers to that question will run thematically through all the chapters of this book.

Competence—being very good at what you do—is part of that relationship, as are integrity, veracity, dependability, and availability. Cooperation and honesty are two important strands in the relationship. Both competence and cooperation are integral to the relationship of trust, and that relationship is strengthened by integrity, veracity, dependability, availability, and honesty.

How can this reality, this kind of trust, become part of the life of a corporation? It begins with persons, and it has to begin with the small things—the courtesies, the reliabilities, the acknowledgments, and a genuine institutional humility. In the person of the CEO—the occupant of the corner office—there must be what the philosopher Dennis Goulet in a conversation with me has called "availability, accountability, and vulnerability." Any executive who has been in the corner office will understand what Goulet means by vulnerability. Any effective CEO will agree that availability and accountability belong in the successful executive's toolkit.

Two additional considerations might be helpful. You cannot afford to wait until trust is lost to begin thinking about the maintenance and preservation of trust in your organization. Preventative measures in preserving organizational trust are always less costly and more effective than waiting for a crisis to arise and then deciding to deal with it.

The other consideration is captured by Al Golin, who coined the term "trust bank" forty years ago, and who more recently wrote *Trust or Consequences: Build Trust Today or Lose Your Market Tomorrow*. Golin says: "Just as you wouldn't go without health insurance because you're physically fit, you shouldn't go without a trust bank just because your organization has good values." And what is a trust bank? "As the name implies, a trust bank involves making deposits of good deeds into an account over time that can be drawn upon in times of need."[12] This suggests that the organization should be doing "good deeds" for its employees, its clients or customers, and in its surrounding community. Organizational generosity can build organizational trust.

Put yourself in any present or future workplace environment and think for a moment of all your associates in that place, all those who work in your organization. And think of them within the framework of trust. Recognize that your organization cannot operate without social trust, without the social collaboration of human beings. "The way you create trust," says Kenneth Dunn, dean of the business school at Carnegie Mellon, "is to have complete transparency of your decisions."[13]

Is yours—the place where you work or want to work—a high trust, low trust, or no trust organization? Listen to Francis Fukuyama, whose 1995 book *Trust: The Social Virtues and the Creation of Prosperity,* reminds you:

> While people work in organizations to satisfy their individual needs, the workplace always draws people out of their private lives and connects them to a wider social world. That connectedness is not just a means to the end of earning a paycheck but an important end of human life itself. For just as people are selfish, a side of the human personality craves being part of larger communities. Human beings feel an acute sense of unease . . . in the absence of norms and rules binding them to others, an unease that the modern workplace serves to moderate and overcome.
>
> The satisfaction we derive from being connected to others in the workplace grows out of a fundamental human desire for recognition. . . . [E]very human being seeks to have his or her dignity recognized . . . by other human beings. Indeed this drive is so deep and fundamental that it is one of the chief motors of the entire human historical process. . . . This kind of recognition cannot be achieved by individuals; it can come about only in a social context.
>
> Thus, economic activity represents a crucial part of

social life. . . . [O]ne of the most important lessons we can learn from an examination of economic life is that a nation's well being [I would substitute, "a corporation's well being"], as well as its ability to compete, is conditioned by a single, pervasive cultural characteristic: the level of trust inherent in the society [or, as I would suggest, "the level of trust inherent in the corporation."].[14]

Sir Geoffrey Chandler, former director of Shell International, pointed out in a letter to the editor of *The Economist* (February 5, 2005) that there is a "prevailing public distrust of companies arising from the perception that profit precedes principle, rather than being based upon it." The chapters that follow will highlight the principles, which, if internalized, can contribute to the long-term viability of the capitalist system. "Capitalism," continues Chandler, in his letter to the editor, "the most effective mechanism the world has so far known for providing goods and services and creating wealth, is under threat not from without, but from itself and from its lack of underlying principles."

Trust is one way of summarizing the principles outlined in the following chapters of this book. The point is to identify the principles, understand them, and internalize them. If they are not part of the makeup of persons who populate the corporation, the corporation will not be a principled organization. If your organizational workplace is a caring community built on a foundation of mutual trust, you will be conducting your affairs at an ethical altitude far above the minimalist horizons of "corporate compliance." You also will be a happier human being.

I will end each chapter in this book with an image intended to summarize a central idea. In this instance, I offer below an image that can help shape your idea of culture. The notion of culture is important to the purposes of this book because, as Roger Lowenstein noticed, "it is a chief lesson of the scandals that the culture of a community, more than any laws, provides the moral determinant for its behavior. The customs that govern how executives, auditors, and bankers do their jobs, interact with each other, are motivated, and so forth, ultimately lead to specific deeds or misdeeds."[15]

Imagine a fish bowl.[16] *Everything in that bowl, besides the fish, is the culture. Like air that is breathed by creatures on dry land, the water in the bowl conditions the life of the fish. Pollute the water, and you can kill the fish. Change the water too abruptly, and you might lose some of the fish as a result. Now, put the world of business in that bowl, and you'll begin to appreciate the need for a life-sustaining culture that is purified by the proper values. You might also notice the danger of shifting too abruptly from old values to new ones.*

CHAPTER TWO

The New Corporate Culture

I would like to begin with a story that highlights some of the attractive features of what many are calling our new corporate culture. The ugly features will get plenty of attention; the brighter side should not be overlooked.

This story could possibly have come from the U.S. Postal Service, Fed Ex, or any one of a large number of organizations that deliver greetings and packages at Christmastime. It happens to come from United Parcel Service (UPS), the company that runs those big, boxy, brown trucks on highways and streets all over the country and around the world. This is a story about a UPS driver, Rene D'Agostino, making her routine rounds just a day or two before Christmas on a military base known as the Aberdeen Proving Ground in Maryland.

Michael Eskew, chairman and CEO of UPS, tells the story with great pride, using it to illustrate the central features of his company's business culture.[1]

The military base was fairly empty on that day several years ago, Eskew notes, because most of the military personnel were on Christmas leave. Rene D'Agostino found herself trying to deliver a UPS overnight letter with no specific address, just a name on the envelope. She asked a few people on that sprawling base if they recognized the name; no one did.

Then, Eskew explained, the driver called her UPS supervisor to ask if she could open the envelope to look for some clue as to the recipient's whereabouts. All she found inside was a money order and a handwritten note: "Make me happy. Come home for Christmas. Love, Mom."

The driver figured it out. The money order was there to pay for the soldier's trip home. But where was he? She drove to the on-base house of a Marine officer. He did not recognize the name but agreed to open his office and run a computer search. Sure enough, he located the Marine and identified his barracks. So, accompanied by a Sergeant-at-Arms, the UPS driver entered the barracks, but her man was not there. One of his buddies said he had gone to the Rec Center on base. Off went Rene to find him. He was there, sitting on a couch, surrounded by a stack of rented movies. Apparently, a movie marathon was going to get him through a lonely Christmas.

"I've got something for you," said Rene, and she handed him the opened envelope. He read the note, smiled, sprang off the couch, hugged the driver, and started for the door when he remembered the videos. He turned back to Rene and asked her for one more favor—could she drop those movies off at the Rec Center rental counter for him? She delivered. She also exemplified some of the characteristics of the new corporate culture: speed, mobility, attention to the customer, use of independent judgment within a system of accountability.

Young professionals in the world of business are settling into a new corporate culture, new at least when compared to the one that welcomed newcomers to business back around 1950 and for two or three decades after that. Loyalty to the organization is taken far less seriously now; lifetime employment with the same employer is part of no one's career plan. It was interesting to note that the headline over Erin White's "Managing Your Career" column in the *Wall Street Journal* (www.wsj.com) on March 29, 2005, read: "Savviest Job Hunters Research the Cultures of Potential Employers." The story relates how "corporate-culture clashes are an increasingly common predicament these days" causing individuals to hop "back and forth among companies with radically different attitudes toward everything from dress to management style and conflict resolution."

A culture, as I indicated earlier, is a set of shared meanings, principles, and values. Values define cultures. Those who hold the same values form an identifiable culture. "Hold" is the operative word there. People tend to cling to, commit themselves to, buy into, and share over time a set of meanings and values that shape their culture.

CORE VALUES AND PERIPHERAL PRACTICES

Terrence E. Deal and Allan A. Kennedy write that a "shared narrative of the past lays the foundation for culture." "The trick," they say, "is to maintain core values while altering peripheral practices to deal with contemporary issues."[2] Deal and Kennedy note that a "robust culture in a cohesive enterprise is committed to a deep and abiding shared purpose," and they go on to quote Lee Walton, a former managing director of the consulting firm McKinsey & Company, who says that culture is what "keeps the herd [of employees] moving roughly west."[3]

This is all the more important now that we are in a knowledge economy, where, as Charles Handy says so well, a "good business is a community with a purpose, not a piece of property."[4] In a knowledge economy the assets are often invisible, hidden between the ears of the people who populate the organization. Employees have to share and stick together; the culture of the place provides the glue. Not to be overlooked in a knowledge economy, located in a world of skyscrapers and concrete canyons, the real assets of more than a few major businesses go down the elevators and out the door at the close of business every day!

The old corporate culture in America featured, as I said in the last chapter, values like freedom, individualism (often of the "rugged" variety), competition, loyalty, thrift, stability, fidelity to contract, efficiency, autonomy, self-reliance, power, and profit. The structure was vertical; the style was command and control. It has yielded to a new horizontal structure with a style that stresses communication and cooperation. Speed, facilitated by the Internet, is everywhere, and "everywhere" presents itself in the garb of globalization. Today's business leader stands in the center of a widening circle, not at the top of a power-based pyramid.

Many of those same old values are still prominent in corporate America, although they are interpreted now somewhat differently.[5] There are some new values emerging to define the new corporate context. In the old days, rank and power shaped the organization. Today, "mutual understanding and responsibility" are needed.[6] Newcomers to management ranks will have to cultivate an understanding that is indeed mutual, and practice responsibility by bringing to life within themselves a personalized ethic of responsibility.

Back in 1977, Robert K. Greenleaf first published his seminal work, *Servant Leadership*. In the early pages of that book, Greenleaf provides what I view as a descriptive bridge between old and new in business culture, acknowledging that all of the old is not yet gone, and all of the new is not yet here:

> A fresh critical look is being taken at the issues of power and authority, and people are beginning to learn, however haltingly, to relate to one another in less coercive and more creatively supporting ways. A new moral principle is emerging which holds that the only authority deserving one's allegiance is that which is freely and knowingly granted by the led to the leader in response to, and in proportion to, the clearly evident servant stature of the leader. Those who choose to follow this principle will not casually accept the authority of existing institutions. *Rather they will freely respond only to individuals who are chosen as leaders because they are proven and trusted as servants.* To the extent that this principle prevails in the future, the only truly viable institutions will be those that are predominantly servant-led.
>
> I am mindful of the long road ahead before these trends, which I see so clearly, become a major society-shaping force. We are not there yet. But I see encouraging movement on the horizon.[7]

True, we are not there yet, but there is a noticeable managerial step down from what I referred to above as "the top of the pyramid" and movement toward the "center of the circle."

The new corporate culture is very comfortable with the notion of "stakeholder." The term is a play on the more traditional "stockholder," but the play is made to point to a range of interests far beyond owner interests that require allegiance and ethical attention. This is a sign of ethical maturity. The outlook is more communitarian, closer to the common good.

"The Organization Man" could be found anywhere in American business after World War II. "The Man in the Gray Flannel Suit" had a Madison Avenue address in the 1950s. IBM's famous dress code back then, and for several subsequent decades, was the dark suit, white shirt, and quiet tie. John K. Waters, in *John Chambers and the Cisco Way,* observes how styles had changed when Chambers, an ex-IBMer who "fairly glowed with the aura of IBM," arrived at Cisco Systems in 1990:

> In the entrepreneurial meritocracy of Silicon Valley, established old-line technology companies like IBM had been the enemy, your father's company, a place where individuality was squashed and conformity ruled. All of that had been discredited in the land of T-shirt millionaires. The perception of success had changed. Some people in Silicon Valley went to work without *shoes,* never mind a necktie.[8]

Dress codes, *per se*, have nothing to say one way or another about ethical behavior; they just point to the possibility of culture shifts.

WHEN THE EMPLOYMENT CONTRACT
BECOMES THE BUSINESS PLAN

John Thomas started out as a manufacturing manager with Johnson & Johnson in 1963. Four years later he joined the management consulting firm Booz Allen Hamilton. Eventually, he formed his own management consulting firm; when I caught up with him for an interview in 2004, he could look back over thirty years of work with top-level executives. He shared with me some observations that provide an interesting marker for an end of the "old" and the beginning of a "new" corporate culture. "At the beginning of client assignments back in the 1960s and 1970s," he said, "we always asked to see the company's business plan and usually got a fairly detailed and well-thought-out document describing the management's vision of the future and how they were going to get there. Their employees organized their departments around these plans. By the late 1980s, when I would ask for a business plan, the CEOs would usually unlock their desks and give me a copy of their employment contract and say something like, 'the business plan is on page 25.' "

This veteran business consultant then went on to say, "Compensation plans had become the business plan, not the reverse, and the worst of this began to surface in the late 1990s. Worse yet, it has not abated." He admitted to a pessimistic outlook on the quality of contemporary corporate life. "Too many of today's managers are self-indulged, materialistic, spoiled brats who feel they are just plain 'entitled' to whatever they want without sacrifice or responsibility," he said.

One noncontroversial way of examining what is "new" in the new corporate culture is to look through the lens of employment contracts (written or unwritten). Let me begin the examination this way. Question: What's the difference between getting fired and being downsized? Answer: About fifteen years and a new corporate culture.

People have been getting fired since hired hands were first employed to extend an owner's reach and productivity. But now there is something new in the old reality of layoff or separation from payroll. In that "something new" lies the difference between firing and downsizing. There is more to the difference than a simple distinction between blue and white collars. Today's wilted white collars were never so plentiful, and their wearers' hopes for quick and permanent reinstatement have never been so thin. But there is more to it than that.

Typically, organizations are "downsized" at the end of a process that has come to be known as de-layering, restructuring, or reengineering. The machine-tool metaphors veil the psychological trauma felt by men and women who are set adrift. Fifteen years ago or more, they went out one door and entered another around the corner, down the street, or in some not-so-distant place where anyone who was "looking" could find a job. Now the looking can go on for years until either a new opportunity (often at less pay) can be found—or until a psychological darkness, a deep discouragement, sets in to signal the end of the search.

Those who bounced back quickly not all that long ago were leaving organizations that were not shrinking, just experiencing turnover. The corporations or organizations around the corner and down the street had not shrunk either. Turnover there meant opportunities for job seekers from outside. This was before the days of what *The Economist* of London, in describing the American economy a little more than a decade ago, called "corporate anorexia."

Multiplication of managerial positions used to be taken for granted as technology developed, markets expanded, and the economy grew. Now technology keeps on expanding, many old markets (and lots of new ones) continue to grow along with the economy. But layers of management, like so many rugs, are being pulled out from under the well-shod feet that, until recently, walked with confidence along the corridors of corporate America. Now they are out and looking; many could be looking for quite awhile unless they understand themselves and the new corporate culture.

As their organizations shrink, displaced managers themselves have to expand personally. They have to enlarge their outlook and their personal ensemble of employable skills. Self-assessment, along with a careful inventory of what one can bring to a new employer by way of value added, is step one into the next career stage. With that step, however, the job seeker is moving into a new corporate culture where a new corporate contract may be on the table. Survival in next-stage careers requires that rebounding managers understand the new culture and contract.

That new corporate contract is now explicitly contingent—no job is forever. There was an *implied* contingency in earlier arrangements, which might be thought of as relational contracts, even though both parties to corporate employment contracts thought and acted as if the relationship would continue uninterrupted straight through to retirement. Now the contracts, written or unwritten, that define work relationships within organizations are more transactional than relational; not quite as transactional as the contract between a house painter and the owner of the property, but today's employment contracts are offered and received with a clear understanding that contract and career are not coextensive terms.

There is much more, of course, to the new corporate culture than just the employment contract. I have emphasized the employment dimension simply because the downsizing hammer has fallen on so many good people over the past fifteen years and has been noticed by just about everyone. In · their often long and painful transitions back to work, transitioning managers noticed a lot of change and not all of it good.

THE SHORT-TERM OUTLOOK CAN LEAD TO MORAL MYOPIA

Long-term versus short-term is another way to compare old and new corporate cultures. "My long-term game plan for the short-term world," reads the text above the picture of a young woman in an advertisement for SAP, which appeared in the business press in the summer of 2003. The ad gives the reader no help in figuring out what SAP purports to be. Upon inquiry, I learned that SAP stands for "Systems, Applications, and Products in Data Processing," and I presume that it is a business systems software company offering customers a tool to deal with the short-term mania that characterizes the new corporate culture.

In a news report at a recent business conference, there was an old-corporate-culture tone in the concern voiced by both Warren Buffett and the Wilmette, Illinois, Ethical Leadership Group. They agreed that "extremely high short-term incentives can distort long-term business performance."[9] Breaking away from a fixation on near- or short-term results is another way of viewing separation from the values of the old corporate culture.

University of Pittsburgh business law professor Douglas Branson suggests that one benefit that might emerge from the Enron debacle is an end to the "winner's culture." This is another way of describing the "new" emphasis that emerged in business in the 1990s. It was reinforced by the stock option craze and precipitated regulatory reaction. An editorial writer for the *New York Times* sees the elimination of stock options at Microsoft as a sign of "a change in business culture"[10] that could be a signal of a return to sanity.

The "software civilization" is one headline writer's description of the new corporate culture, and that, I think, says it well.[11] If you trace the sweep of the software business from the 1960s up to the present, you get caught in a blur of new company names, new products (including software itself becoming a stand-alone product), and completely new ways of doing things in business. Here, in the sprightly language of *Time* magazine (March 29, 1993), is how the new corporate culture was beginning to look:

> Companies are portable, workers are throwaway. The rise of the knowledge economy means a change, in less than 20 years, from an overbuilt system of large, slow-moving economic units to an array of small, widely dispersed economic centers, some as small as the individual boss. In the new economy geography dissolves, the highways are electronic. Even Wall Street no longer has

a reason to be on Wall Street. Companies become concepts and in their dematerialization, become strangely conscienceless. And jobs are almost as susceptible as electrons to vanishing into thin air.

The "conscienceless" characteristic broke into full view in the early years of this new millennium.

It is a "new world of uncertainty and risk," says a *Business Week* cover story,[12] and that was true even before September 11, 2001.

What else is new? Along with the World Wide Web and the Internet, there is the revolution in molecular biology and all of its implications for medicine and business. Speed and change are characteristics of the new corporate culture; no one seems to have enough time anymore. The difference between analog and digital, remarked Jack Valenti, then president of the Motion Picture Association of America, is what Mark Twain might describe as the difference between "lightning and the lightning bug."[13] All of this has implications for morality.

In a book called *Integrity*, Yale law professor Stephen Carter makes this observation:

The lack of time is an unfortunate characteristic of today's Americans, and volumes have been written about how it is hurting our children and our families, but it is hurting our morality just as much. For if we decide that we do not have time to stop and think about right and wrong, then we do not have time to figure out right from wrong, which means that we do not have time to live according to our model of right and wrong, which means, simply put, that we do not have time for lives of integrity.[14]

The walls have come down between commercial and investment banking leaving some ethical rubble that is part of the new corporate culture. Greed, avarice, creative accounting, and similar terms point to something new and troublesome out there in that land of career opportunities for the young, who are a significant portion of the audience this book wants to reach.

"Good people stuck in a bad system" is the way former Securities and Exchange Commission (SEC) chairman Arthur Levitt describes the honest professionals who are trying to keep their heads above the ethical waves in the brokerage industry. They have four problems, says Levitt: (1) bad training; (2) the system is still geared to volume selling; (3) firms give their brokers incentives to sell securities investors do not need; and (4) supervisors, "who are paid commissions just like their brokers, have an incentive to push everyone to sell more and to turn a blind eye to questionable practices"[15]

QUESTIONABLE TONE AT THE TOP

Stephen M. Cutler, director of the Division of Enforcement at the SEC, spoke on December 3, 2004, at the Second Annual General Counsel Roundtable meeting in Washington, DC. This is a gathering of the top lawyers from major corporations. He recited impressive numbers of SEC enforcement cases in recent years and even more impressive dollar values of penalties levied against corporations. "But it's a recitation of the names (and not the numbers) that I think best conveys a sense of the period [the previous two fiscal years] we've just been through." After listing by name about 100 executives and corporations, Cutler continued:

> It takes your breath away. But what does this have to do with tone at the top [the title of his presentation]? One of the connections is probably obvious to everyone here: that is, in so many of the cases I've just cited, the tone at the top couldn't have been all that ... well, pretty. Indeed, in the last two plus years, we have sued in the neighborhood of 100 public company CEOs. And if CEOs were themselves breaking the law, then they couldn't have been setting a particularly melodious tone.

And Cutler continued:

Violations of the securities laws are very frequently the product of both individual failings and a deficient corporate culture. Among other things, a complex accounting fraud rarely can be accomplished by one or two rogue employees, acting alone. . . . We're trying to create an environment that reduces the risk of misconduct at all levels of a company—an environment in which the people who run public companies will do more than simply keep themselves out of jail.

In short, we're trying to induce companies to address matters of tone and culture. We're trying to get the fundamentally honest, decent CEO or CFO or General Counsel—the one who doesn't break the law—to say to herself when she wakes up in the morning: "I'm going to spend part of my day today worrying about, and doing something about, the culture of my company. I'm going to make sure that others at the company don't break the law, and don't even come close to breaking the law."

Given this description of some of the problems in the business culture that today's MBA graduates and other young professionals are encountering, what kind of protective gear can they be expected to wear to work? Here is Cutler's suggestion to the corporate lawyers:

From an employee's first day on the job to the day he gets his gold watch, he should know that ethics and honesty are important at your company. And how should he know that? Because you've told him so. Every company—it really should go without saying—must have a strong code of ethics and a set of written policies and procedures to enforce and reinforce those standards.

If those moving up in management in these post-Enron days hope to change a corporate culture for the better, they will have to do what they can to change the dominant values they are likely to encounter there. This is not an easy task. It calls for strength of character and principled behavior. And where do they come from?

"In life, I have found that there are basically two ways a child develops into a principled and ethical adult: by having a positive adult role model to emulate or by seeing the ugly side of human nature and disdaining it." These are the words of Frank Taylor, a senior marketing representative for the computer company Cybersystems, who gave an interview to Joseph L. Badaracco, Jr., for his book *Leading Quietly: An Unorthodox Guide to Doing the Right Thing*,[16] Not all would agree that exposure to the "ugly side" is necessary, but it does present a learning opportunity, and, all would agree, such opportunities have been plentiful in recent years. Even more plentiful, it must be acknowledged, are the positive adult role models in and out of business who can help to shape the character of the young.

This book hopes to facilitate an understanding of the necessary principles. The wisdom and example of seasoned veterans—positive role models—of the business world is also presented in these pages and will speak more effectively than my words in clarifying the principles. Ideally, in my view, those on their way up should be talking with those who are in place and ethical, as well as those on their way out (or already retired), about the ethical traps that this new corporate culture will spring on the unwary.

Young people, observes John Gardner, do not assimilate values by learning definitions. "They learn attitudes, habits and ways of judging. They learn these in intensely personal transactions with their immediate family or associates. They learn them in the routines and crises of living, but they also learn them through songs, stories, drama and games. They do not learn ethical principles; they emulate ethical (or unethical) people."[17] This is not to suggest that definitions are useless, or that the printed page has nothing to contribute to the learning process. It is simply to observe that cold print without human interaction is insufficient. The necessary ethical principles cannot be learned without first observing them in the lives of others.

Improvement in the ethical environment of corporate America will happen if newcomers and tested veterans get close enough together for the values of the elders to be caught by those who are inexperienced but willing to learn. The point of this book is to offer some common ground for the meeting of their minds.

―――――――――

The image I would offer at the end of this reflection on the New Corporate Culture is that of a roller coaster. Speed is there. Ups and downs are also there. Think of the rise and fall of Enron, the dot-com booms and busts, the creation of new industries and the crashes of careers. Still there are tracks in place and a supportive infrastructure that we call the U.S. business system. You just have to find the right track and have both compass and courage to accompany you on the ride.

CHAPTER THREE

Integrity

I think of integrity in terms of wholeness, solidity of character, honesty, trustworthiness, and responsibility. Students in the Sellinger School of Business and Management at Loyola College in Maryland pass, as they enter and exit the building, a plaque honoring the memory of the former president of the college after whom the school is named. His admirers thought the following words of Thomas Jefferson caught both the Sellinger spirit and character, and that these words would serve to remind students of the importance of integrity: "In matters of style, swim with the current; in matters of principle, stand like a rock."

Students have to be encouraged to understand that "right is right if nobody is right, and wrong is wrong if everybody is wrong," as Bishop Fulton J. Sheen often put it. Wise words, and always true. But here at the outset, I want to offer a tempering, but by no means contradictory, opinion of Peter Drucker, the management theorist whose integrity and wisdom are widely admired. He once remarked:

> On the one hand, men of strict and virtuous conscience deserve our admiration for their support of unpopular causes. On the other hand, because their conscience refuses to compromise with power in any form, they change nothing, move nothing, and accomplish nothing. Power often corrupts, but the impotence of "pure dissenters" produces casualties instead of results.[1]

If only it were all black and white, life would be a whole lot simpler!

The notion of integrity, it should be noted in the wake of the corporate ethics scandals, needs to be extended beyond persons to include income statements and balance sheets, which, of course, depend on the integrity of those who prepare them for their own integrity.

In a 2004 interview, I asked James E. Burke, former chairman and CEO of Johnson & Johnson, how he understood integrity and how he would define it. He is admired worldwide as a model of integrity for his 1982 decision to pull Tylenol from drug store shelves everywhere after a product-tampering incident in which some Tylenol capsules found to be laced with cyanide caused seven deaths in the Chicago area.

When I asked Mr. Burke to give me his understanding of integrity, he summarized it all in one word: Trust.

> Tylenol was driven by a belief I had. . . . There was no question as to what I had to do, and what the company had to do. There were people in the company who questioned me, and there were those who disagreed with me. But there was no question in my mind. You can't put a product on the market that killed seven people and not take responsibility for it. And the best way to take responsibility for it is to get rid of it and give the public what they should have had in the first place. The Tylenol case is a classic example of where trust worked.
>
> People felt that the company could be trusted when I took that product off the market. I think it was a $56 million business then. That was an enormous sacrifice to make. I think the business now is $1.8 billion. It couldn't have happened, of course, without the fact that the public trusted us and trusted Tylenol. My whole claim in these areas is that trust is not only the only way, but it also works. . . . The reason I stick with the trust thing is that it simplifies it all.[2]

LINGERING DOUBTS ABOUT PERSONAL INTEGRITY

Tests of integrity crop up everywhere in business. Twice in a seven-day series of lengthy articles in the *New York Times* on "The Downsizing of America" (March 3-9, 1996), mention is made of a CBS executive who, ten years after the fact, still had trouble looking himself in the eye in the mirror during his morning shave. He had lingering doubts about his personal integrity.

A young colleague had come to him for advice about buying a house. The manager knew the man's job was targeted for elimination, yet he "felt bound by corporate duty to remain silent." The colleague bought the house, later lost his job, and found himself not only out of work, but trapped with a large mortgage in a declining real estate market as other organizations also downsized. Something closer to the truth than detached silence might have prevented subsequent grief for the subordinate and regret for the executive.

It is one thing to take severe measures to guarantee the survival of the enterprise, it is quite another to deceive others, and even worse, in an environment of corporate downsizing, to reduce employment to improve a balance sheet or boost a stock price.

Ethical reflection would want to follow the dollars carefully for clues to why decisions are made that are adverse to many and beneficial to a few. Following the dollars to trace out the fairness of the dollar distribution is an ethical research tactic that is not new but one with practical currency in the new corporate culture. Arthur Andersen's honesty, integrity, and general competence were all called into question in the wake of the Enron scandal. Andersen's failure to find Enron's accounting flaws, its conflicted relationships with the client, and its alleged cooperation in corporate wrongdoing set off the call for reform that has already affected the whole accounting profession. Persons of integrity never have to cover their tracks on an earnings trail or compensation path that is staked out within ethical guideposts.

Greed can erode integrity. Executive compensation levels that strike objective observers as excessive (some might even say "obscene") should be subjected to an ethical standard traditionally applied to the accumulation of property. How much land can one person own? Is there an ethical limit? Yes there is, and that limit is "reasonable use." Ownership is private, but use is common, according to this theory. The common good is injured if one private owner holds more land than he or she could ever reasonably use. To put it another way, if one person accumulates or "hoards" land that is put to no good use, thus depriving the community of reasonable access to that land, this is unethical.

Now apply that to income. Income taxes should have a redistributive effect; charitable contributions also result in redistribution in favor of those less well off. But even after taxes, income levels can be far above any prudent and reasonable "use" criterion, and there is an ethical obligation to put some of that surplus back into the service of the community. Financial windfalls that come to executives in function of downsizing decisions, for example, should be shared with the victims of downsizing. This is really a question of justice.

UNDERSTANDING INTEGRITY

Back now to the point of one's personal understanding of integrity. If you get that right, you will not find yourself caught in the quicksand of greed. Here is how Charles Watson explained it to me. His book, *Managing with Integrity: Insights from America's CEOs*,[3] prompted me to contact him. This professor of management at Miami University of Ohio took me on a brief etymological tour through the Latin "integer," with its emphasis on "oneness," and "integralis," which translates into a good, strong English adjective, on to the notion of "wholeness" to arrive at a sense of "what one purports to stand for" and what indeed is, in Watson's words, actually "stood up for." He sees integrity as a "consistency between standards espoused and actions taken—especially when no one is looking."

One of my Loyola MBA students, John King, mentioned to me that "integrity comes from the same root as integral and conveys the sense of being a fundamental or nonremovable part of something. For me, this means that I am the same person all the time." "Nonremovable" is a good way to think about it.

It is interesting how others I spoke with emphasized "consistency" in expressing their views about integrity. I interviewed Robert A. Reed in Omaha on September 11, 2003. He is president and CEO of Physicians Mutual Insurance Company. When I asked him to define integrity, he responded: "Absolute, not straddling the fence. A person of integrity must be a whole person, living his or her principled life consistently." Now there's an expression that is worth jotting down—living a principled life consistently.

Think first about having a "principled life" and then think about living it "consistently." Reed remarked, "Once people get to know you and what your values are, there should be no surprises. Consistency in moral conduct and moral decision making brings stability and predictability to the organization you are leading. Others know that their leader has a moral compass against which decisions are made."

The operational "nitty-gritty of everyday life," he said, is "taking a breath when you want to explode, holding your tongue when you want to lash out, and keeping your conduct worthy of your moral compass."

THE BEDROCK OF ALL OTHER BUSINESS VIRTUES

The "best evidence" of a person's integrity, says John H. Bryan, Jr., chairman of Sara Lee, is when you find a person making decisions "based on what's in the best interest of the institution, loyal to the institution and nothing for himself. . . . It's amazing how people around here shy away from the one that you know is making a decision, making a judgment, that he thinks is going to serve him. Or, after he has been misleading a couple of times, he loses, he's gone, he gets out of the mainstream of business."[4]

For Gerry Roche, senior chairman of the executive search firm Heidrick & Struggles, "Integrity is the number one absolute today, a real *sine qua non*, the bedrock of all other business virtues." He told me that when a Wharton School student asked him what to study to prepare for managing well in business, he replied: "Study human nature." Become a student of human nature, and you'll find that there is much to be learned about integrity in both life and literature, he said. When it comes to maintaining integrity in business practice these days, Roche would warn the young manager to "be aware of the gray areas in accounting, be scrupulous about product quality, and be honest with colleagues and subordinates regarding expectations." All of these, he points out, relate to long-range profitability. At all costs, he insists, "avoid short-term expediencies and focus on long-term results."

Taking a practical, realistic, but unexpected turn in his reflection on the meaning of integrity, John Fontana, a veteran business consultant now working almost exclusively for the May Department Stores Company, brought up the question of health. He reminded me that without mental, physical, and spiritual health, even the best intentions will not provide assurances of personal integrity. He recognizes that "following through on commitments" is a good clue to the presence of integrity, and he notes that rigidity and an unwillingness to adapt may signal an integrity problem, but without the "wholeness" of health, integrity will not be solidly grounded in a person in business.

For the reader who might still be asking, what *is* integrity, let me quote Stephen Carter once again:

> When I refer to integrity, I have something very simple and very specific in mind. Integrity, as I will use the term, requires three steps: (1) *discerning* what is right and what is wrong; (2) *acting* on what you have discerned, even at

personal cost; and (3) *saying openly* that you are acting on your understanding of right and wrong.[5]

Carter, too, like the business practitioners I met, expects "the integral leader to display the virtue of consistency," but acknowledges at the same time "how hard it can be to live a life of integrity so understood."[6]

Taking a pass on anything "profound or scholarly" in responding to my question, but drawing on more than four decades of management experience in manufacturing, Myer Alperin, of Scranton, Pennsylvania, told me that he would simply say that "there is no compromise" as his way of explaining integrity. This echoed author and management trainer Larry Johnson's remark that he tells young managers these days to "locate your baseline and don't cross it, and if you don't have a baseline, get one!"

"No chalk on your shoes" is the way Raymond A. (Chip) Mason, chairman and CEO of the Baltimore-based asset management giant Legg Mason, puts it. "They kid a lot about that around here," he told me, "but they all know what it means and that it is to be taken seriously." He was talking, of course, about the baseline, the out-of-bounds line. Step on it, and you have chalk on your shoes.

Chip Mason illustrated the point and principle with a story. "I got a call one day from someone in Louisiana whose name I didn't recognize. He came on strong as if he were an old friend, but I really could not place him or remember ever meeting him. He had a business proposition that gave me some pause, so I told him I'd have to get back to him. I immediately called someone I know well in New Orleans, who I thought might know the caller, and gave him an outline of the conversation. He knew the fellow and said, 'Chip, you know how you're always talking about chalk? Well this guy has chalk on both sides of his shoes! You and he could never work together.' "

Mason says he makes it clear to new associates that "Not only do I not want you to go out of bounds, I don't want you near the line. If you've got chalk on your shoes, you're too close. I don't want you anywhere near the line." He acknowledged that mistakes will be made—"Someone who's never made a mistake is someone who has never done anything. But where I draw the line is: Was it intentional? If it was intentional, that's a whole different story. You are never ever intentionally to do anything wrong. If you do, you roll; you're out."

UNLESS THE PEOPLE DOING THE DEALS HAVE INTEGRITY...

Tom Grzymala is president and CEO of Alexandria Financial Associates, a boutique financial services company in Alexandria, Virginia. Upset by press reports of a $1.4 billion settlement that the SEC worked out with ten Wall Street firms, he sent an e-mail message to all his clients with an attachment of the *Wall Street Journal's* (May 7, 2004) story of a Senate hearing on the settlement. Grzymala's message:

> You may be aware that ten of the country's largest brokerage houses will pay a $1.4 billion fine for leading investors astray. . . . We here at AFA want you to know that we make every possible effort to insure all the stocks and funds we invest your money in are run by honest people. . . . I'll not beat around the bush—honesty is spelled HONESTY. Humans can and do err; none of us is infallible, but the fraud and deceit that shows up virtually every day can neither be tolerated nor accepted. I hate to get on a soap box, but that's the way it is here today at AFA!

It helps a lot in getting at the essence of integrity to view it through the lens of simple, basic, easy-to-understand honesty. One CEO, speaking of his chief financial officer with whom he occasionally plays golf, said to me, "If he were to move a ball in the woods, and no one saw him do it, he'd take an extra stroke. If I had to rush out of the office to catch a plane, I'd sign anything he handed me that I hadn't had the chance to read." That may be more a tribute to trust than prudence, but the point is clear.

Novelist Zoë Heller's character in *What Was She Thinking?* uses the word "mendacity" in a context having nothing to do with Wall Street but surely applicable to major malpractitioners there: "For some people, honesty is such an unusual departure from their standard *modus operandi*—such an aberration in their workaday mendacity." Workaday mendacity is simply incompatible with organizational integrity.

The SEC has over the years had many concerns with the way America Online (AOL) booked its marketing expenses. Robert O'Connor, the AOL vice president for finance, aware of past problems, responded to one of the company's internal accountants who asked what might be done to prevent future problems, by saying, "You can have the greatest controls in the world, but unless the people doing the deals have integrity, it doesn't matter what the hell you do."[7]

In another matter, an SEC settlement included lifetime bans from the securities business for two analysts—Jack Grubman of Citigroup Inc.'s Salomon Smith Barney securities unit and Henry Blodgett of Merrill Lynch. They were accused of misleading investors by issuing overly optimistic research reports on certain stocks to win investment-banking business for their respective firms. (For more on Grubman, read *Business Week*'s August 5, 2002, cover story, which takes you "Inside the Telecom Game" and explains "how Salomon's Jack Grubman wheeled and dealt with WorldCom, Qwest, Global Crossing, and others," as insiders made millions while the industry collapsed.)

ON WHICH OTHERS MAY RELY

In a booklet entitled "Creating and Maintaining an Ethical Corporate Culture,"[8] the Woodstock Theological Center's Seminar on Business Ethics laid out some basic values, explaining what they are and why they contribute to an ethical culture within which to conduct business. One of those values is honesty, and here is a short paragraph from the booklet that describes it:

> Honesty requires the avoidance of deception and careless misrepresentation of information on which others may rely. Communications, both internal and external, should be truthful and accurate. Care should be taken, for example, to ensure that accounting, financial reporting, and marketing efforts are not misleading. Honesty also calls for directness and candor with colleagues and openness to inquiries from legitimate constituencies, insofar as compatible with the obligations of confidentiality and with other responsibilities. In some cases, honesty may require specific disclosures, so that affected parties will have access to relevant information.[9]

The phrase "on which others may rely" puts a pillar under the principle of integrity. In business, countless others—customers, suppliers, employees, competitors—are relying on the honesty of those who put products, services, or information out there for the public to buy or use. As Grzymala would put it, "People are counting on you. All the letters have to be there—and in the right order—for all to see, so that whatever you say or do in business does, in fact, spell HONESTY!"

Let me take a moment here to prepare you for an editorial speed-bump on your reading road. I am now going to place you into a time machine that will roll you back to the 1960s. A brief quiz awaits you below. Some of the numbers will seem dated (because they are), some of the language may seem quaint, but all of the questions will, I believe, prove to have stood the test of time and remain close to the mark.

In a 1962 article in *America* magazine,[10] business management professor Raymond J. Murphy of Wayne State University challenged parents to check their own "Integrity Quotient" before criticizing a growing tendency in the young to participate in academic dishonesty. To facilitate this check-up, he attached the following questionnaire to his article:

What's Your "Integrity Quotient"?

Your Business Relationships (after each question, mark a Yes or No response):

1. Do you violate proper office-hour procedure by arriving late, or leaving early, or by taking lengthy lunch periods or coffee breaks?

2. Do you pad your business expense accounts by overstating mileage, hotel, food, telephone items, etc.?

3. Do you participate in business practices that might be classified as "kickbacks," "under-the-table payments," or "bribing"?

4. Have you ever claimed credit at work for the ideas or labors of someone else?

5. Do you "borrow" stamps from the office supply for personal use and then forget to pay for them or replace them?

6. Have you received benefits through improper reporting relative to welfare relief, unemployment or workmen's compensation, or GI dependency?

7. Have you placed the blame on someone else for your own mistakes at work?

8. Do you use company time or facilities (telephone, car, office, etc.) for personal business?

9. Do you pass off most of your responsibility to colleagues to free yourself for your own personal pursuits?

10. Do you take "approved leaves," ostensibly for company business or sickness, when, in fact, they are for personal reasons?

11. Do you take meals in public places, or pick up magazines or newspapers at stands, and walk off without paying?

12. Do you entertain (at the theatre, sports, etc.), or give gifts to your personal friends or family, and then charge it to business expense?

13. Do you ever claim credit for overtime work at the

office or for time spent away from the office "on business" when, in fact, it is otherwise?

14. Do you knowingly order merchandise for a specific purpose and then return it after it has served its purpose?

15. Do you take home and keep office supplies or equipment for your personal use?

16. Have you knowingly accepted overpayments in change from merchants without returning it?

Your Private Relationships (after each question mark a Yes or No response):

1. Have you claimed income-tax deductions by improperly listing a child, parent, or other dependent?

2. Have you circumvented government rationing procedures* on gas, food, etc.?

3. Have you cheated at sports, such as tennis, golf, or at cards, crossword puzzles, etc.?

4. Did you try to beat traffic laws through speeding, illegal turns, parking violations, etc.?

5. Do you shortchange the government on your income-tax return by overstating charitable deductions, interest payments, retail taxes paid, medical payments, etc.?

6. Have you used connections to "fix" traffic violations?

7. Do you sponge on your neighbors by using their TV, consuming their drinks, their snacks, etc., without any attempt to reciprocate?

8. Are you a "seat jumper" at theatres, sports events, etc. (buy a $2 seat* but occupy a $4 seat)?

9. Do you sometimes find yourself "tapping" the house funds or the kids' "piggy bank" without returning the "loan"?

---

*Do the references to government rationing and two-dollar tickets in this 1962 questionnaire stir up a bit of nostalgia? If so, later references in this chapter to Broadway of the 1940s will also be nostalgic.

10. Do you sometimes connect your outside home electrical appliances, water, etc. to your neighbors' outlets?

11. Do you tell your spouse that you are out with the boys (for men) or girls (for women) when, in fact, it is otherwise?

12. Do you cheat your spouse by overstating home operating-expenses (for women) or normal incidental work expenses (for men)?

13. Do you frequently use someone else's automobile without any thought of paying for or replacing the gas used?

Jackpot Question:

Have you answered any of the above questions with a "no," when in your heart you knew it should be "yes"?

Scoreboard: "Yes" answers to questions in either group (plus the Jackpot Question) should be rated thus: zero rates an A (Excellent); 1-2 gets a B (Fair), 3-4 merits a C (Weak but Satisfactory); 5 and over rings up a D (Failure).

Let the reader not lose heart. The rest of this book will help you improve your score!

AN EYE FOR HUMAN WEAKNESS

When playwright Arthur Miller died (February 14, 2005), the *New York Times* editorialized on the "Death of a Legend" and took the occasion to point out the relevance of Miller's early work to the corporate scandals at the time of his death. "Mr. Miller wrote drama that . . . unabashedly did battle with villains like corporate malfeasance—the subject of 'All My Sons,' in which a military manufacturer knowingly sells defective parts, causing the deaths of American pilots." The writer of the signed editorial, Adam Cohen, knew Miller personally and relates that they were together at a small dinner party in 2002 when someone asked Miller if any of his plays were especially popular just then. "Mr. Miller had a grin on his face when he said he was flooded with requests to revive *All My Sons*. The news had been full of Enron and WorldCom, and, Mr. Miller said, people could smell the corporate mendacity in the air."

This sent me back to re-read *All My Sons*, which opened on Broadway on January 29, 1947. In Joseph Mersand's introduction to the published version of the play, I found these words that speak to the issue of integrity: "What so impressed and edified both the critics and the audience on that opening night in 1947 still shines through the pages as one reads the play today, more than fifteen years later. The moral judgment that the play expresses about the businessman who places his personal aggrandizement above his responsibility to the rest of mankind is as cogent in 1964 as it was in 1947; and it has been throughout human history."[11]

Similarly, in Miller's most famous play, *Death of a Salesman*, the tragic collapse in the character of Willy Loman is caught poignantly in words spoken by Willy's wife Linda, who, aware of Willy's downward spiral of discouragement and eroding self-confidence, pleads with their two sons, Happy and Biff, to show their father more respect. "He's the dearest man in the world to me," she says, "and I won't have anyone making him feel unwanted and low and blue." And to Biff, her son who has lost all respect for his father, Linda says: "Biff, I don't say he's a great man. Willy Loman never made a lot of money. His name was never in the paper. He's not the finest character that ever lived. But he's a human being, and a terrible thing is happening to him. So attention must be paid."[12] Willy needed the oxygen of affirmation, a point to be kept in mind by those who ignore their own character flaws and fail to see the human weakness in tragic figures.

Miller was 33 when *Death of a Salesman* opened on Broadway. At age 68, he said in an interview with the *New York Times* that he could see himself in the character of Willy Loman: "Willy's writing his name on a cake of ice on a hot day, but he wishes he were writing in stone. He wants to live on through something. . . . I think all of us want that, and it gets more poignant as we get more anonymous in the world."

Correct and quick as we are to condemn violations of integrity, compassion for the violators should prompt us to be willing to pay the "attention" that could prevent the lapses and to give the affirmation that all of us need if we are going to stand up to reality when the pressure is on to cut the corners or take the easy out.

Let me begin the closeout of this consideration of integrity by referring to Robert Bolt's play, *A Man for All Seasons,* based on the life of Thomas More, who faced execution in the Tower of London for his refusal during the reign of Henry VIII to swear to the Act of Succession. More's daughter urged him to "say the words of the oath and in your heart think otherwise."

But More says, "When a man takes an oath, Meg, he's holding his own self in his own hands. Like water. [*He cups his hands.*] And if he opens his fingers then—he needn't hope to find himself again. Some men aren't capable of this, but I'd be loathe to think your father one of them."

Margaret replies: "In any State that was half good, you would be raised up high, not here, for what you've done already. It's not your fault that the State is three-quarters bad. Then if you elect to suffer for it, you elect yourself a hero." And her father replies in words that speak to the heart of anyone striving for integrity in contemporary corporate America:

> That's very neat. But look now. . . . If we lived in a State where virtue was profitable, common sense would make us good, and greed would make us saintly. And we'd live like animals or angels in the happy land that needs no heroes. But since in fact we see that avarice, anger, envy, pride, sloth, lust and stupidity commonly profit far beyond humility, chastity, fortitude, justice and thought, and have to choose, to be human at all . . . why then perhaps we must stand fast a little—even at the risk of being heroes.[13]

And that is the risk that those just starting out in business will have to be prepared to take.

None of this is far removed from the reality of contemporary business life. One who understands that reality well is Fred Hassan, chairman and CEO of the pharmaceutical company Schering-Plough, who wrote: "In the end, business success is not about numbers. It is about building trust. You must develop mutual trust among the people in your organization for everyone to do his or her best. An essential element of trust is being truthful. And when you have the trust of your customers and shareowners, you have an exceptional competitive advantage."[14] And he continues:

> I use the term "business integrity," rather than "business ethics," for a reason. In my experience working across many cultures, the language of "ethics" can unintentionally be divisive. It can imply that one culture's "ethics" are better or more profound than another's. By contrast, I have found that that business integrity is something that people around the world can understand and own. In many ways, business integrity is also a broader concept than ethics. I explain it very simply to the people I lead in a complex, global industry. Business integrity means living up to the intent, and not just the letter, of the laws and regulations wherever we operate. It also means more. It means obeying the internal moral compass that we all have, so that in each situation we face in our business life, we consciously choose to do what we believe is right and reject what we believe is wrong. There will always be shades of gray in life, but we must evaluate them and make our choices in line with the direction of this internal compass.

WATCH YOURSELF GO BY

Bill Glavin's internal compass served him well as vice chairman of Xerox and later, upon retirement from business, as president of Babson College. He is convinced that integrity "is one of the few things in life that no one can take away from you." If you want to, you can give it away, he says, but you should "have enough confidence in yourself and your ability to quit a job if someone wants you to give up your integrity."

An unusual management principle that he has carried with him since learning it in 1955 from Tom Watson, Sr., at IBM, is this: "Step back and watch yourself go by." Glavin explains: "What it means is once every three or four weeks, stop and review what has been going on in your life—in both your personal and business life. Review the things you have been doing and determine if they are what you should have done. Or, are there other things that would have been more useful that you should have done? It takes only 20 or 30 minutes and it is really worth the time." Periodic reflection like this is, in Bill Glavin's experience, not only useful in practical matters, but more than helpful in preserving and protecting your integrity.

As one who believes, and has often remarked, that "one good apple can save the barrel," I was struck by Harvard Business School Dean Kim Clark's use of the apples-and-barrel metaphor when, on February 26, 2003, he walked into the lion's den of a National Press Club luncheon to speak about business ethics and corporate misconduct. He began by saying,

> Two broad classes of explanation [of the scandals] are out there. One puts primary responsibility on a few bad apples and sees the solution as catching them, prosecuting them, putting them in jail, fining them—whatever is appropriate. That's one pole of this continuum. But the other pole has people who believe there's something extremely wrong with the barrel; that it's not just a matter of a few bad apples, but we really need a wholesale revamping of the systems of governance ... that the solution is to remake the barrel with a lot of new legislation and a lot of new regulation.[15]

To no one's surprise, Clark saw "elements of truth" at both poles but found more truth and hope for a solution "somewhere in between." The problem, he thinks, is that a good economic system which has "become an engine of progress and development unmatched in the world," has also become "so complex, and its capabilities so swift and powerful, that it has outstripped the governance mechanism designed in a simpler time."

While reaffirming his commitment to a free market system, Clark mentions markets as part of the three problem areas that need attention:

(1) "As markets have become more pervasive, firms have used them badly;"

(2) "We have seen leaders substitute market-based incentives for judgment and for standards;" and

(3) "We have seen governance institutions compromising principle in the pursuit of market opportunity."

Clark, who is now president of Brigham Young University, cited problems with executive compensation, board compensation committees, consultants who advise boards on compensation, auditors, investment analysts, and rating agencies. "[W]hen the institutions no longer provide clear guidance and a framework for action, individuals are faced with competing demands, and the potential for wrongdoing, even the temptation for wrongdoing, is much stronger."

The individuals are the apples; the institutions form the barrel. So where does the search for a solution lead?

> Markets—and this is a really important idea that I think we may have lost sight of—markets require faith. They require trust and faith in the integrity of data and information and the reliability of promises. Even more, they depend on the existence of principles and standards and well-understood rules that define how the system operates. To work, they require leaders who understand the importance of integrity in the creation of trust, and who inspire that trust in their people, their organizations,

and in the communities and the larger society of which they are a part.

So, the search for a solution will take you, in effect, through the markets to the decision makers within—toward integrity of data and integrity of persons within the system.

We need leaders who are prepared to act on principle, with standards and values to guide them, even in the face of strong financial incentives to do otherwise. In fact, we need a lot of those kinds of people throughout the system. It is perhaps a paradox that in order for a market-based system to really work effectively, you need a lot of people whose behavior and action is not based on the market, but rather on standards and principles that help that market function.

In summing up, and just before opening himself up to the famous slings, darts, and skeptical inquires that typically follow a presentation on any topic to a Press Club audience, Kim Clark said:

In the world I see ahead, a world of turbulence and uncertainty, where there are opportunities that are fraught with risk and reward, we need leaders with strong values. We need leaders who place a high value on excellence, on building organizations where people thrive, on creating long-term value for customers and for investors. We need leaders who understand the larger purpose of the enterprise and the principles and standards that derive its success. We need leaders whose behavior matches and reinforces those values. And that is what I mean by integrity. Integrity is more than being honest, although it certainly means that. It is deeper. It is about the match between what the leader says and what the leader does. Leaders with integrity have strong values and standards and principles, and they act on them—consistently, without fail in public and in private. Such leaders inspire trust and confidence in those around them, and the values they espouse become reality in the organizations they lead, because people act on them and live them in their organization.

Predictably, the first question, from a reporter whose identity and alma mater are unknown, was: "How much responsibility should business schools like Harvard take for the corporate scandals of the past few years?" The Harvard dean acknowledged that it was a "good question," and said, "Each one of us has a responsibility." He did not, however, reference that responsibility to past failures, only toward a present recommitment to the school's mission of bringing "principle, and standards, and values to business."

The moderator, reading from the card on which another question was written, announced that this one came from "a Harvard Business School graduate, who had a classmate there who is now a convicted felon. [That classmate] 'oozed integrity at Harvard,' this questioner says." The moderator continued, reading from the card, "Machiavelli said that leaders should appear to have all the values you espouse, but not actually follow them when it's not expedient. How do you know you're not just training students in managing appearances?" (The transcript notes that the question drew laugher.) Clark gave a lengthy reply outlining a "whole series of things that we do," ranging from admission procedures, to the organization of the school, and the example of faculty, "the materials we create, the classroom discussions—it's a total experience to make sure we do everything we can to help our students understand the importance of these issues, and really believe in them as an important part of what they do." The objective, of course, is to foster the development of character.

Throughout this book there will be occasions to mention the importance of character, which, of course, is easily associated with integrity. Speaking on "Bedrock Values for Shaky Times: Business Ethics Revisited" to a Stanford Business School audience (October 15, 2002), Sidney Taurel, the chairman of Eli Lilly and Company, told the students and their professors that he had come across a good definition of character in a story of how the National Football League runs a training camp for rookies in an effort to prevent them from various forms of self-destruction in the high-paid, fast-paced world of professional football. The players are told that "character is what you do when you are angry, afraid, or bored . . . and no one is watching."

Elsewhere in this book I outline how secrecy, easy money, and the violation of trust define a framework for the test of character in the world of business.

The image I would like to post at the end of this chapter on integrity is the surveyor's plumb-line, or the plumb-bob at the end of a line held in the hand of a member of a surveying crew. The weighted bob seeks the center of the earth, and the string between bob and fingers holding the string represents a perfectly upright line against which a wall under construction can be measured for its uprightness. The vision of the prophet Amos (7:7-9) employs this image to measure the integrity of the nation Israel. If the nation is "out of plumb" (dishonest, not straight), it, like a leaning wall, will eventually collapse. With new surveying technology, plumb-bobs are used less frequently now, but the image is a good one. Other images, some from the building trades, catch the meaning and spirit of integrity: on the level, up and up, straight arrow. Enron and Arthur Andersen "collapsed," which is to say, they failed to meet the plumb-line test.

CHAPTER FOUR

Veracity

I recall years ago in Washington coming out of a Senate committee hearing on organized crime and stepping into the elevator in the Dirksen Senate Office Building with the committee's general counsel. We had just been listening to extended testimony from a veteran, straight-as-an-arrow, state police chief. As the elevator doors closed, the counsel remarked, "My father told me long ago that anyone who always tells the truth doesn't have to worry about having a good memory. That's what you just witnessed in that hearing room today."

Integrity means living truthfully. Veracity means speaking truthfully. Veracity is truthfulness, and the truth will always set you free. There may be unpleasant consequences for you if you tell the truth. But, as the saying goes, "the truth will always out," and the truth teller will always have a place to stand, a soul to claim, and a peace of mind that can never be taken away.

Truth not just when convenient, truth in all circumstances is the only compass that works in an age of ambiguity. The truth teller is, we like to say, "trustworthy." He or she is a person you can count on, whose word is always good, whose character is the pledge behind the claim. A lie, for such a person, matches up well with the concise Latin definition of a lie employed by medieval scholastic philosophers: *locutio contra mentem*. The "locution," or external expression, is contrary to what the mind knows to be true, and that is unacceptable behavior. Forgetful or confused persons are not necessarily liars when what they say is inaccurate; the problem is in their minds, not the words or gestures that are consistent with their confused, uninformed, or misinformed minds.

The ad copy produced by Madison Avenue for Wall Street firms or other business advertisers would have the public believe that there is character behind proclamations of principle on the part of organizations that claim to put the public's interest ahead of corporate profit, personal advancement, or institutional preservation. After Enron, the public will not be easily misled. Certainly, the instinct for self- and organizational preservation runs strong throughout the new, as well as the old corporate culture. Today, however, all stakeholders, especially those whose jobs are in jeopardy, should be told the truth in matters that are likely to affect their livelihood. This does not usually happen. Deceit is often the forerunner of abrupt layoffs. When the axe falls suddenly, you can presume that others of the old ethical principles, like the right of participation and the principle of personal dignity, were violated. Truth telling, as difficult as it may be at times, is the only way to preserve an ethical corporate culture. In this sense, veracity reinforces all the other principles under examination in this book.

AN UNWILLINGNESS TO LIE

I spoke about this with Ralph Lancaster, a wise, experienced, veteran lawyer from Portland, Maine. He told me, "Veracity and truthfulness are twins. Implicit in conformance to fact is a commitment to accuracy and honesty. But I think you establish confidence in a person's veracity if you can get that person to state it negatively and simply say that he or she is committed to 'an unwillingness to lie.' " Now there's a good way to think about veracity—simply as an unwillingness to lie.

The circumstances in which that kind of commitment will be tested in business are multiple. One simple example was communicated beneath a *Baltimore Sun* headline on Decem-

ber 7, 2004. It read: "Fired CEO Linked to Cooked Books."
It was a story about Richard M. Scrushy, the ousted chief
executive of HealthSouth Corporation, who was accused by
his company's former chief financial officer, William T. Owens,
of being at the center of a scheme to overstate earnings. Scrushy
personally directed his subordinates to report per-share earnings at $1.00 in 1999, twice as high as they actually were
according to Owens, who pleaded guilty to participating in
fraud and was cooperating with the government with an eye
to emerging from his predicament with a lighter sentence.
Scrushy faced federal charges of fraud, conspiracy, and false
corporate reporting, all related to intentional misstatements
of earnings. Inflated revenue figures meant higher stock prices
to meet market expectations, please shareholders, and make
the exercise of stock options more attractive. Scrushy, the
government charged, forced his subordinates to lie, and they
(and this is a test of personal character) were not unwilling to
follow orders. Scrushy was later tried in Birmingham, Ala-
bama, and found to be not guilty on all counts.

Junior employees at Kmart were transferred or demoted
"when they resisted a manager's demand in 2001 to incorpo-
rate numbers they believed to be unrealistic into the company
forecasts and reports," according to newspaper accounts of
an internal investigation conducted by an outside law firm.[1]
They clearly paid a price for their unwillingness to lie.

John Coughlan, a seasoned veteran in the world of accountancy, runs the CPA School of Washington. He told me that
he tends to think of veracity as a subcategory of integrity. He
said that the codes of ethics of the American Institute of Certified Public Accountants (AICPA) and of several state societies of CPAs and state boards of accountancy have "a provision that members must practice accounting with 'integrity,'
but they don't say members have to tell the truth!" He then
went on to ask:

Does "integrity" mean that the practitioner has never
broken one of the Ten Commandments and has never

done anything evil? I very much doubt it. CPAs, myself included, no longer have the high ideals that drove them when they were cub scouts and brownies. I have always thought that integrity meant two things: that the CPA told the truth; and that the CPA was good at distinguishing between his money and the other person's money.

When I asked Coughlan for his views on the causes of the corporate scandals, he replied:

My perception of the causes of the management and accounting scandals of the past few years is that, except for the very few who take vows of poverty, we are victims of greed. We know the truth of Tolstoy's dictum that the amount of land a man needs is six square feet, but none of us are content with that and we all want more land, more stocks, more bonds, and more net worth. We know that a fancy car, a large home, and a big tombstone are nothing but vanity, but we still want them. The cupidity of managers, accountants, and analysts blinds us to integrity, fairness, and veracity. Way down deep we know what's fair, and what's honest, but we seek a law, a rule, a FASB [Financial Accounting Standards Board] statement that permits us to do what's convenient, what's expeditious.

With admirable candor, Coughlan went on to say that he had served, shortly before I contacted him in 2003, as a seminar leader for an AICPA course on accounting principles. In that capacity:

I excoriated SFAS 142 [a provision dealing with financial accounting and reporting for acquired goodwill and other intangible assets] as an invitation to "earnings management" which the AICPA, SEC, and FASB all condemn, while remaining, in my view, complicit in earnings management. At the break, one of the participants, a practicing CPA, came up to me and said he hadn't known about SFAS 142, but that it sounded like something that gave him an opportunity to improve the reported income of one of his clients. And I proceeded to say, "Yes, and here's how you do it." Can you imagine! Both he and I were thinking of how he could improve his standing with management when both of us should have been thinking what course of action was most useful to inform the stockholders and creditors of what was happening to the company. Driving home from the seminar, I realized my error; but did I make an effort to contact the practitioner? No.

A CRUCIAL BUT NEGLECTED VIRTUE

One of several avenues to an understanding of the importance of truth telling for Shep Abell was growing up around his family's business; they were publishers of the *Baltimore Sunpapers*. Accordingly, he carried a heightened sense of sensitivity for accuracy and truth telling into the practice of law. Now a senior partner in the firm of Furey, Doolan & Abell, in suburban Washington, DC, Shep Abell told me that he finds himself correcting a tendency that some young associates have to say, in written or oral communication with clients, "It's almost ready," when, in fact, not one word for the brief or memorandum has found its way onto any page anywhere. "Veracity is a crucial but neglected virtue," says Abell. "It is easy to start with small untruths, but it can escalate into exaggeration of the number of hours worked (and billed) for a matter, and outright misrepresentations to or on behalf of a client." Roger Lowenstein made essentially the same point in the final paragraph of *Origins of the Crash*: "[W]e should not be surprised if in a culture that tolerates lying, even in seemingly marginal ways, public reports and disclosures become unreliable."[2]

A month or two later, Abell sent me an article he clipped from the March 24, 2005, issue of the *Wall Street Journal*.

The headline over Sue Shellenbarger's "Work & Family" column read: "How and Why We Lie at the Office: From Pilfered Pens to Padded Accounts." "Amid the uproar about top executives cooking the books, another ethical meltdown has gone largely unnoticed," writes Shellenbarger. Acknowledging that "corporate culture does shape employee truthfulness," the article documents cases like the one of a human resource director who says her boss is so demanding that she lies to cover instances when she misses meetings or refuses business trips because of family responsibilities. She wants her boss to believe that she "is as much a workaholic as he is." The article goes on to make this interesting point: "But any lie has hidden costs, not only in teamwork and productivity, but in an employee's own self respect. Once you start stretching the truth, it's easy to forget where to stop. The human resources director also pads her travel-expense reports, adding an occasional extra meal or inflating the amounts a bit, to help cover the high cost of child care while she's on the road."[3]

A direct tie between veracity and customer relations was impressed upon Martha Sloboda, a regional manager for a medical manufacturing company called Adhesives Research, by these words of her company's founder, which she passed on to me: "Talk straight and do what we say we are going to do."

Dan Geer, formerly chief technology officer for @Stake Inc., is one of the most knowledgeable consultants I know in the business of helping banks and other businesses defend themselves against computer fraud. He says that the best (i.e., most effective) way to lie is to omit. Hence, the truthful person will not allow falsehood to be created in the mind of the listener through one's own omission. Veracity, he told me, "requires that the past be remembered as it was, and the present be described as it is. You must, in short, forget how to lie." As for the future, Dr. Geer, whose Cambridge, Massachusetts, firm is known as Geer Risk Services, thinks the future should be described in a way that matches promises with particulars that are clearly identified as your own best guess, your humble opinion.

Another way of saying that the "best way to lie is to omit," is to speak of "selective information." "Can Truth Be Told When Using Selective Information?" asks Jeffrey L. Seglin in his *New York Times* column "The Right Thing" (August 17, 2003). His point of departure is David Mamet's play *Glengarry Glen Ross*, where cutthroat competition among real estate salesmen has them doing whatever it takes to sell property to the unsuspecting, "even if that means being selective in what you disclose about the houses you want to unload." Their cultural mantra is "always be closing."

"Let the buyer beware" is an ancient defensive guideline in the marketplace, and we have grown accustomed to politicians using selective information in campaign speeches and both policy and program announcements. The principled person who truly wants to "forget how to lie" cannot take the easy exit of selective information. Being ethical, to state the obvious, is not always easy.

VERACITY IS A FOUNDATION FOR INTEGRITY

A book worth reading is Sissela Bok's *Lying: Moral Choice in Public and Private Life*. "Never to Lie?" is the title—note the question mark—of Chapter 3. The range of complexity associated with lying is signaled, however, by this sampling of other chapter titles: "Is the 'Whole Truth' Attainable?" "White Lies," "Lies in a Crisis," "Lying to Liars," "Lying to Enemies," "Lies for the Public Good," "Lies to the Sick and Dying."

Without getting into dilemma ethics and questions best left to case studies for classroom debate and discussion, I will note three points that Bok touched upon that merit consideration by those hoping to keep their integrity and credibility on a high level in business: (1) there is a distinction that some find useful between intent to say what is false and intent to deceive, the former to be avoided, the latter permissible in certain circumstances; (2) in a situation where an innocent human life can be saved by a lie, not normally the case, of course, in business, "non-maleficence, or the avoidance of harm, would be the principle invoked, and most would hold that it overrides the principle of veracity in these cases [crisis situations where individual choice can avert an evil outcome]. Just as force would be justifiable as a means to prevent murder, so it would be right to achieve the same objective through deceit." And (3) Bok ends her book with these two sentences: "Trust and integrity are precious resources, easily squandered, hard to regain. They can thrive only on a foundation of respect for veracity."[4]

Respect for veracity will turn a reflective person's attention to the need for discretion, in the view of Ken Sparks, former executive director of the private sector Federal City Council in Washington, DC. He and his organization serve as patient and honest broker between private business interests and public officials for the translation of visionary ideas into huge projects that serve the economic advancement goals of the national capital area. One good example of a Federal City Council project that worked is the Washington metropolitan area subway system known as the Metro. In any case, Sparks knows the importance of the link between veracity and discretion and stated it for me in these words: "Where you know something to be true, but when asked, are not in a position to release the information, you have to be prepared to practice discretion."

Dr. Charles M. (Chuck) Geschke co-founded, with John Warnock, Adobe Systems in 1982. He still serves as chairman of the board of the San Jose, California, software giant, although he retired from day-to-day operating responsibilities in 2000. Geschke has a great respect for veracity. When I asked him for his views on the whole range of ethical principles covered in this book, he replied with an expression of strong interest and encouragement, saying that "the cascade of business failures and the loss of trust in corporate leadership troubles me greatly." Instead of responding to specific questions, he preferred to give me a copy of an internal memorandum he circulated to all Adobe employees shortly after the firm was challenged with a hostile takeover attempt in the summer of 1998. Appended to this paper is a two-page list of

"Adobe's Core Values and Beliefs." I will be mining that memo here and elsewhere in this book.

Geschke's paper was intended as a description of how all the employees of Adobe "should think, feel, behave, and represent this corporation." The essay, he explained to me, was offered in August 1998 to help all employees focus on the most important principles and values that had built the company. It is a "business built with intellectual capital," he said. "Adobe's strong financial balance sheet is not based upon assets such as factories, warehouses, storefronts, or mining or mineral rights. The capital assets of our corporation are our people. . . . Therefore, how we behave and operate, i.e., our culture, as an organization, has direct impact on the financial success of our business." In this context, veracity is essential to the health of the business. Geschke was direct, even blunt, in making his point by focusing employee attention on two values—trust and honesty.

> Trust: Without trust, [my] earlier comments on teamwork and leadership are worthless. In order to trust someone you must know them. I have observed an insidious habit recently where groups or individuals are criticized by others who have not taken the care to investigate the facts that are used to support the criticism. This behavior erodes trust, which in turn disables teamwork. Unless we improve corporate-wide communication to provide the necessary information upon which accurate assessments can be made, we will not be able to build the level of trust required to effectively operate our business.
>
> Honesty: The most important virtue of Adobe's corporate culture is honesty. The only sure-fired way to be asked to leave this organization is to knowingly fail to tell the truth. This attribute of our culture requires no further explanation.

Michael Jordan, chairman and CEO of Electronic Data Systems (EDS), sees honesty as the *sine qua non* of successful business leadership. "Countless studies have been conducted on leadership over the years. Results typically reflect behavioral characteristics such as 'you have to be aggressive' or 'you have to present well.' My point of view is that the only characteristic you need is honesty. Everything that's important springs from honesty."[5]

Other leaders in business and law offer similar advice to their associates, as well as to students and newcomers to professional life. A good example of this is Fred Weisman, senior attorney at the Cleveland law firm of Weisman, Kennedy and Berris, speaking to 200 students and scholarship donors at a Case Western Reserve University Law School luncheon on April 22, 2003. He was commenting on the recent proliferation of corporate fraud: "Without our good name, we are essentially worthless. We're nothing. And that is true if you have twenty million bucks in your pocket. You're nothing."[6]

EVIDENCE OF MENDACITY

Investment analysts have learned the hard way that a negative comment in an off-hand e-mail message to a friend that contradicts a positive buy recommendation offered earlier for a particular security is not just a simple lapse of judgment; it is evidence of mendacity. "UBS Analyst Is Forced Out for HealthSouth Remark" reported the *New York Times* on July 3, 2003. UBS, a global financial firm, fired its top health care analyst, Howard C. Capek, when bank officials discovered an e-mail message in which he bad-mouthed HealthSouth ("What a mess; I would not own a share") shortly after he had given the stock the highest possible rating. This is the same problem that brought down Merrill Lynch's former Internet analyst Henry Blodgett. Both analysts worked too closely with their respective firms' investment bankers. The *Times* notes that "while there is no explicit evidence that connects Mr. Capek's cheerleading coverage of HealthSouth to the banking work" of Benjamin D. Lorello, UBS's top health care banker, "UBS bankers arranged over $2 billion in deals with HealthSouth while Mr. Capek covered the stock."[7] Regardless of the motivation, a lie is still a lie. That's why it is good for individuals, and the firms that employ them, to have an internalized principle of veracity operating on automatic pilot all the time.

"Lying may be a sin, but on Wall Street there has always been a spirit of understanding for those who merely help others to deceive—particularly because the fees for aiding in deception have often been far higher than those for simply arranging a straightforward financing."[8] Financial writer Floyd Norris is referring here to a "new morality" that is intolerant of past banking practices that permitted loans to be booked as investments, thus disguising a borrower's debt. Four former executives of Merrill Lynch went on trial in Houston for, the prosecutors said, providing phony profits to Enron by disguising a loan as payment for Nigerian barges.

Norris's use of the word "sin," by the way, prompts me to recall St. Basil the Great's definition of sin as "the misuse of powers given us by God for doing good." Men and women in business have an extraordinary range of powers for doing good; when used badly, those powers are no longer virtues, just tools for unworthy purposes. For example, accounting standards are powerful tools in the hands of an auditor. If an auditor permits a client/company to classify certain debts as long-term rather than as current liabilities, this helps the company understate its current obligations and overstate its working capital, thus enabling the company to mislead investors.

Don Aucoin's "Currents" column in the Boston *Globe Sunday Magazine* (August 10, 2003) highlighted New York State Attorney General Elliot Spitzer's disclosures of the extent of fraud committed by Wall Street investment banking firms; the article bears the title "Let's Be Honest." "The country seems to be on a lying binge," writes Aucoin. "The simple act of telling the truth seems unaccountably hard for a lot of people these days, even though covering the tracks of a falsehood often lands the liars in even hotter water." The point to be noted is that "the simple act of telling the truth" is a solution to the problem of corporate fraud. "The tide of corruption at Enron, WorldCom, Tyco, Arthur Andersen, ImClone, et al," says Aucoin, "represents a profound breach of the social contract and persuasive evidence of a systemic, robber-baron ethos at play—one that, if unchecked, could threaten the livelihoods and retirement dreams of millions of working stiffs." The way to check it is, once again, "the simple act of telling the truth."[9]

But it is not always that simple. Raymond C. Baumhart, S.J., used the subscription list of the *Harvard Business Review* to gain access to top business leaders for his study many years ago of business ethics in executive suites across America. He found that most of his respondents said they thought that it was harder to know the right thing to do than to actually do it.[10]

EXECUTIVE RESPONSIBILITY CARRIES AN OBLIGATION TO BE COMPETENT

Although I have not presented "competence" as an ethical principle for chapter-length consideration in this book, there is an ethical obligation to be competent—very good at what you do—if you hold a position of executive responsibility. Not only do the careers and retirement security of a lot of "working stiffs" on a given CEO's payroll depend on it, the safety and satisfaction of those who meet the CEO's product or service in the marketplace presume competence to be there on the other side of the exchange. Incompetence is a form of lying. In one-on-one encounters, it is usually evident. But in large organizations not knowing the "right thing to do," or not being able to tell the truth because the matter is too complicated to understand, is a deficit to be overcome before the "simple act of telling the truth" can come to the rescue.

I sometimes think of "competence" as an ethical principle that has received insufficient attention in the nation's hand-wringing search for solutions to corporate corruption. There is, indeed, an ethical obligation to be competent if you hold a job at or near the top of any organization. To repeat: Incompetence is a form of lying. There are a lot of incompetent people behind the corporate scandals of recent years—brilliant in some respects, but incompetent in important areas of leadership responsibility. Not to narrow the range of incompetence just to ethics and accounting, it can surely be said that "The Hall of Shame" would include CEOs who knew nothing about ethics and directors who knew nothing about accounting.

Competence, of course, means mastery; it follows upon days, weeks, usually years of study and practice. Competence is not a gift; it is an achievement. Competence comes only to those who are willing to work for it. Directors who consider board membership an "honor" and executives whose position at or near the top is viewed as an "entitlement" hold titles that are almost always unsupported by the competence required to do the job.

The notion of competence figured prominently in a dialogue on corporate leadership at the University of Notre Dame, April 14-16, 1980. Elmer W. Johnson, then a senior partner of Kirkland & Ellis, a 250-member law firm with offices in Chicago and Washington, DC, was one of the speakers. Johnson mentioned that he had been assigned by his firm to write up a set of criteria by which partners in the firm might be measured over the long term for compensation purposes. He viewed the criteria as describing his "ideal of a top partner of a large law firm, which, with a few modifications, describe my ideal of a top executive of a large corporation." At the top of the list is professional competence. He described it in these words:

> The partner will be measured first and foremost on the basis of technical competence in the partner's particular field of expertise, peripheral vision in perceiving legal problems outside the partner's field of expertise that call for attention of others in the firm, readiness to seek from

and provide others in the firm such professional consultation as will serve the clients' best interests, and creativity and imagination in solving client problems.

I should add that the other listed criteria were: personality and cooperation, judgment, productivity, leadership, and external representation. Johnson explicitly presumed moral character to be associated with each criterion. And in spelling out in a bit more detail his understanding of competence, Johnson said, "First, the pursuit of competence calls for self-discipline. It has been my experience that the top lawyer or corporate executive or leader in any other organization who has a high degree of competence is a person who is slightly monastic. The self-indulgent hedonist is unlikely to develop great competence."

In giving advice to Catholic Church officials trying to work their way through the clergy sex-abuse scandals of 2002, Margaret O'Brien Steinfels, former editor of *Commonweal,* said simply, "Tell the truth. . . . We must pursue a form of what Vaclav Havel, president of the Czech Republic, called 'living in truth' in his 1978 essay, 'The Power of the Powerless.' 'Living within the truth,' he wrote, 'is an attempt to gain control over one's own sense of responsibility.' "[11] Havel saw "living a lie," as a condition, says Steinfels, "so subtle, and so unconscious that those who live a lie may not fully grasp the ordinary subterfuge in which they carry on their daily life." Havel's point, she noted, is that people may not believe in the principles of the Soviet system and the Communist ideology, "but they must behave as though they did, or they must at least tolerate them in silence, or get along well with those who work with them. For this reason, however, they must live within a lie. They need not accept the lie. It is enough for them to have accepted their life with it and in it. For by this very fact, individuals confirm the system, are the system."

The subtlety of it all is what those who plead agnosticism about doing and saying the right thing in business have to respect. "Living within the truth" implies a serious responsibility to surround yourself with some factual and ethical education. If *locutio contra mentem* defines the lie you want to avoid, then you need to have both the principles and the facts. You have to make sure that your external expression (the "locution")—either oral, to be heard in words the listener can understand, or visual, seen by the beholder in the written words, gestures, facial expressions, or nods of the truth-telling communicator (you)—is an accurate reflection of what you know in your *mens* (your mind) to be true. Consistency comes into play here; recall the connection with consistency made by some in describing their understanding of integrity in an earlier chapter.

THE DEFINITION OF EARNINGS

To bring this discussion back to the practical ground of everyday decision making in business, I want to take some thoughts from a *Business Week* cover story with the attention-grabbing title, "Fuzzy Numbers: Despite the Reforms, Corporate Profits Can Be As Distorted and Confusing As Ever. Here's How the Game is Played."[12] Principled participants can be in the system without playing the game, but they have to be smart enough to understand the game, and sufficiently grounded in ethics to avoid being taken in by it. The "game" focuses on the definition of earnings.

There is a difference between *earnings* that companies report under the tight rules of so-called "generally accepted accounting principles" (GAAP) and figures for "operating income" that companies publish in their annual reports and press releases. Big gaps between announced income, on the one hand, and earnings reported under stringent GAAP requirements, on the other, tell a story that investors should be attending to. But investors tend to react to the press releases. Much of the Enron story can be told in terms of what the company failed to disclose in announcements of its operating income.

In the Haliburton case, *Business Week* reported that the giant construction company and military contractor, "did something mind-boggling last year: It reported earnings of $339 million, even though it spent $775 million more than it took in from customers." Nothing illegal was done, which is not to say that nothing unethical happened. The way this game is played permits earnings to be susceptible to manipulation. Presumably, unsuspecting investors will be misled.

It seems that Haliburton made heavy expenditures in 2003 in anticipation of payments from the military for work done in Iraq. However, it booked some of those expected revenues immediately. Only later did investors get the full picture "when the company filed its complete annual report with the Securities & Exchange Commission. Haliburton says it followed generally accepted accounting principles (GAAP)."[13]

Accounting rules grant fairly wide discretion in counting estimated income as earnings; it is called accrual accounting. "By accruing, or allotting, revenues to specific periods, they aim to allocate income to the quarter or year in which it was effectively earned, though not necessarily received. Likewise, expenses are allocated to the period when sales were made, not necessarily when the money was spent." And the report continues, "The scandals at Enron, WorldCom, Adelphia Communications, and other companies are forceful reminders that investors could lose billions by not paying attention to how companies arrive at their earnings."[14] The more important issue, of course, is the need for integrity and veracity on the part both of those who report the earnings in the first place and those outside auditors who certify those reported figures to be in conformity with GAAP.

Some managers will fudge the earnings number to hit previously set targets for their bonus compensation. But even where no bad motives are at work, the complexity of the financial reporting system is enough to cause problems. There are three major financial statements: the balance sheet, the income statement, and a statement of cash flow. According to *Business Week*, "Accounting games are spreading beyond earnings reports as some companies start to play fast and loose with the way they account for cash flows. That's a shocker because investors always believed cash was sacrosanct and hard to trump up. Now they're discovering that cash is just as vulnerable to legal manipulation as earnings."[15] Note that the manipulation is legal.

As for Haliburton, the *Wall Street Journal* reported on January 6, 2005, that the company changed its "system for estimating procurement costs under enormous contracts to support U.S. troop deployment in Iraq." Modification was necessary because a Pentagon audit found that "Haliburton's Kellogg Brown & Root [KBR] unit didn't properly account for more than 40% of the costs billed to the government for services such as housing and feeding troops." An audit in August 2004 faulted KBR for failing adequately to estimate the cost of its work and document its costs. As the *Journal* explained, the company "is reimbursed for its expenses and then receives a small percentage above that for profit. As the scope of the contract expanded quickly, KBR was caught by surprise and many of its internal control systems were overloaded." No criminal wrongdoing was alleged.

Joseph M. Langmead, a CPA who is a retired KPMG partner, explained to me that the audit literature regarding fraud identifies three circumstances that are usually at work when fraud occurs: pressure, opportunity, and rationalization. "These unoriginal ideas are nevertheless valid," he remarked, "and the first of them—pressure—is often as important as greed in explaining why fraud happens." He added that the pressures created for public companies in general "by the quarterly financial reporting cycle often challenge the skills (and ethics) of the best managers."

Companies can legally inflate or deflate the earnings they report in several ways: by sales estimates, prediction of bad debts, inventory adjustments, forecasting unusual gains or losses, and massaging cash. Containing the legal within the broader circle of the ethical is a managerial responsibility. At the end of the *Business Week* article previously cited, the editors ask: "What to do?" And they answer:

> Companies should make sure all the estimates and judgments in reported earnings are transparent. They should simplify their financial statements to make them clear and comparable. And at the least, they certainly need to report income and cash flow for the same time periods. Clarity and honesty in accounting would not only make the financial markets more efficient but also might head off a second round of corporate scandal and regulation. Does anyone want Sarbanes-Oxley, Part II?[16]

TRANSPARENCY, CLARITY, HONESTY

Whether or not you think Sarbanes-Oxley was a good development, you will surely agree that transparency, clarity, and honesty in accounting will raise veracity to a new and higher level in the American business system. If you are wondering whether a reasonable measure of veracity might have been able to prevent the collapse of Enron, consider these words of Arthur Levitt, former chairman of the SEC:

> Enron's collapse was brought on by the collision of all the unhealthy attitudes, practices, and conflicts of Wall Street and corporate America that I tried to address at the SEC. It was as if everything I feared might happen did happen—within one company.
>
> Enron used accounting tricks to remove debt from the books, hide troublesome assets, and pump up earnings. Instead of revealing the true nature of the risks it had taken on, Enron's financial statements were absurdly opaque. Auditors went along with the fiction, blessing the off-the-books entities that brought the company down. Most analysts also played along, recommending Enron's stock even though they couldn't decipher the

numbers. Analysts were foils for their firms' investment banking divisions, which had been seduced by the huge fees Enron was paying them to sell its debt and equity offerings.[17]

Without a general appreciation of so-called "mark-to-market" accounting, and its potential for abuse, the Enron fraud would be difficult to understand. Bethany McLean and Peter Elkind point out that before joining Enron to run a new "Gas Bank" division for that company, Jeff Skilling (who eventually became Enron's president and chief operating officer before serving as CEO from February to August 2001, when he abruptly resigned) insisted that the new business would have to use mark-to-market accounting, instead of historical cost-accounting. "Because much of what happened at Enron can be traced to the decisions to use mark-to-market accounting, it's important to take a moment to understand it," write McLean and Elkind, who then go on to explain, "When you use conventional accounting, you book the revenues and profits that flow from [a ten-year contract to supply natural gas to a utility] as they come through the door. But under the mark-to-market method, *you can book the entire estimated value for all ten years on the day you sign the contract.* Changes in that value show up as additional income—or losses—in subsequent periods."[18]

Why was Skilling so interested in a particular accounting method? "He felt that a business should be able to declare profits at the moment of the creative act that would earn those profits."[19] McLean and Elkind then note that if one takes this line of thinking to an absurd extreme, you would say that "General Motors should book all the future profits of a new model automobile at the moment the car is designed, long before a single vehicle rolls off the assembly line to be sold to customers. Over time, this radical notion of value came to define the way Enron presented itself to the world, justifying the booking of millions in profits on a business before it had generated a penny in actual revenues."[20] It is obvious how badly investors could be misled by such reported "earnings." Originally, Enron used mark-to-market accounting only for reporting on its natural gas futures contracts. But by 1997, "Enron had extended mark-to-market accounting to every portion of its merchant business. It even began using the approach to book profits on private equity and venture-capital investments, where values were extraordinarily subjective. By the end of the decade [of the 1990s], some 35 percent of Enron's assets were being given mark-to-market treatment."[21]

There were many more tricks that Enron pulled out of its accounting bag, but the numbers booked as mark-to-market income were in such a stratospheric range, with no solid grounding in reality, that they stretched veracity beyond all reasonable and ethical limits. As Ralph Lancaster would have told anyone at Enron who might have bothered to ask, "Veracity and truthfulness are twins; in combination they amount to an unwillingness to lie." And, as Joe Langmead reminded me, "Accounting standards are agreed-upon human constructs providing ways of measuring those relevant things which can be measured with sufficient objectivity. Even when scrupulously applied, much 'truth' about the company remains unmeasured and unspoken."

Think of a clean and clear see-through window as a takeaway image for veracity. The image itself suggests transparency, and it recalls a story from the rabbinical tradition called "The Window and the Looking Glass," which can touch both mind and heart of anyone who finds "the system" closing in on them. A century or more ago, a man unburdened himself to a wise rabbi, disclosing feelings of discontent and unhappiness. The rabbi walked the man across the room to a window and invited him to look outside and tell him what he saw. "I see people moving up and down the sidewalk," he said. Then the rabbi invited him to look into a mirror that hung on the office wall and again asked the man to report what came into view. "I see myself," was the reply. Gently then, the rabbi pointed out that the only difference between the window and the looking glass was that the glass in the mirror was coated with silver. "If you scrape away some of the silver from your life, you will be able to see others as you did when you were younger, become concerned now about their needs, and you will find happiness once again." Good story. Good image for veracity. Good reminder that "the truth will set you free."

CHAPTER FIVE

Fairness (Justice)

Everyone knows what fairness is. Just walk by a children's play area and listen to the shouts of, "No fair! No fair!" We have an inner sense of fairness, and we know when an unfair advantage has been taken. At least we think we know, and we are usually convinced that we are absolutely right. We just know it! Sometimes, a few additional facts or the recognition of our own biases will prompt us to reset our fairness clock, but we have a way of just *knowing* when unfair treatment occurs.

Similarly, when we call it "justice," we are talking about treating equals equally, giving to each what is his or her due. A lawyer friend reminded me that the fairness issue arises frequently in deciding how to divide a family's assets in a will. "I believe it promotes a more harmonious family to have things evenly divided," he said, "but there are obviously times when 'equal' is not 'fair.' "

We can visualize justice as lawyers do, as trays in balance on a scale. This imagery keeps the notion of power in close association with the idea of justice. As Barbara Ward once wrote:

To illustrate the degree to which philosophers have long recognized the consequences of unbalanced power, one has only to recall Thucydides, the great Greek historian's account of Athens and Melos. "The human spirit is so constituted that what is just is examined only if there is equal necessity on both sides. But if one [side] is strong and the other weak, that which is possible is imposed by the first, accepted by the second." That is why, since antiquity, the symbol of justice has been a figure holding equally balanced trays.[1]

We can also think of justice as the prophet Amos did, in building-construction terms, as that which is measured by the straight (upright) string connected to a plumb-bob. We cry, "Unjust," when corners are cut, the social structure is "out of plumb," or when things are simply not "on the up and up."

You always have to be careful, of course, to control that tendency, when the scales are tipped against you, to "get even" and to baptize mean-spirited and unfair revenge "in the name of justice." You can trick yourself into believing that avenging yourself by harming those who have harmed you is "right and just." That behavior is both obvious and unworthy; it is clearly inconsistent with your own human dignity.

There are other traps set to spring out there in the corporate jungle. They will always be there, in good times and in bad, putting pressure on both the integrity and a sense of justice of those who inhabit the business system.

There will always be idealists in our midst (and we can thank God for that!) who will keep nudging us toward a realization of a "fair society." One such is Emitai Etzioni, who, from his faculty post at George Washington University, coordinates "The Communitarian Network." He commissioned the Greenberg, Quinlan, Rosner opinion research firm to conduct a public opinion poll from June 28 to July 1, 2003, to discover "whether the yearning for a fair society could provide a unifying theme for society."[2] The survey began with the following statement: "A fair society is one in which nobody is left behind. This is not just a promise, but a new America where anyone who seeks work can get a job, nobody can be cheated out of their pension rights, and all health care is accessible to everyone so nobody will ever have to choose between buying medicine and food."

The survey found that if a hypothetical presidential candidate would take that position, he or she would have strong support from 58 percent of the voters. If the question were asked in a business, as opposed to political context, the issues would be viewed broadly as questions of corporate social responsibility; that viewpoint will emerge in Chapter 9. For the moment, readers of this book might pause to ask themselves how they would describe a fair society, particularly from the vantage point of day-to-day business activity. If you ask around, you will surely get an interesting array of viewpoints on the meaning of fairness and justice in business.

CONSTANCY AND AUTHENTICITY

Carroll W. Suggs, now retired after succeeding her husband as Chairman and CEO of Petroleum Helicopters, Inc., is widely respected in business circles in the Gulf South. She uses the word "constant" often in discussing principled business behavior. In the matter of fairness, she says that it is "the ability to respect all individuals no matter their station in life or relationship, offering each individual the same treatment." The constants she stresses are:

(1) authenticity ("be who you are and be it consistently");

(2) strong personal and professional relationships ("successful organizations are collections of individuals working together with a shared vision toward a common goal");

(3) vision ("if you know yourself and your vision, you can set your direction");

(4) commitment to be the best ("no matter how good you are today, you can be better tomorrow").

In her view, you have to be constant if you want to be fair.

Another female executive, Jeannine Norris, former director of business services for Riddle Memorial Hospital in Pennsylvania, takes a similar approach: "I believe the principle of fairness not only involves treating equals equally, but also treating subordinates fairly and equally." James J. Maguire, Chairman of Philadelphia Insurance Companies, came to an appreciation of fairness through volunteer work he did for the deaf soon after leaving college. He became an advocate for the deaf. "As a hearing person who spoke sign language," he told me, "I worked on their behalf, and this taught me the value of giving. I also learned that fairness and human dignity were often denied them because of their handicap. As a result, I made sure that fairness and human dignity were part of our corporate culture since the day I founded this company."

Larry Herbster is now retired as vice president and general manager of Nextstar Broadcasting of Northeastern Pennsylvania, an NBC affiliate. He has managed broadcast properties in Washington, DC, and Oklahoma City. He factors "reliability and consistency" into his understanding of integrity and, when it comes to fairness, he says it means "being balanced." Explanation: "If there's any doubt about playing favorites on an issue or with an individual, always ask yourself: How would I want to be treated in this situation?"

The notion of balance comes up often in conversations I've had with business executives who are serious about ethical decision making. They want to know how legitimate interests and competing claims can be balanced. After describing the dimensions of a given dilemma, they will often hunch up their shoulders a notch or two, extend their upturned palms, and ask, "How do we bring all this together into some kind of balance?" That always recalls for me two things—an ancient saying and a symbol.

In medio stat virtus is the classic saying from the poet Horace. Virtue stands in the middle. Maintain balance. There is virtue in the middle ground. The image of open palms suggests to me two trays in balance on a scale, the familiar scales of justice. If I take unfair advantage of you, my tray is down, weighted with the unfair gain; yours is up, lighter than it should be and waiting for the action of compensatory justice, a shifting of the weights (*pensa* in Latin) back where they belong—in balance.

Joseph Kraemer, director of the Washington, DC, office of Law and Economics Consulting Group (LECG), specializes in electronic commerce. He views fairness as "never asking your people to do what you cannot or will not do yourself" and acknowledged in an interview with me that this conviction "is left over from my army days, but still applicable in a corporate environment." By way of example, he said, "Whenever work requires extraordinary effort—red-eye flights, all-night sessions, whatever—I make a point of being there with my team whatever it may take for however long it takes."

Dan Geer, the Internet expert, takes a philosophical and almost poetic approach to this question. "Fairness, to be in its fullest flower," he says, "knows that equality is not fair and fair is not equal, and disguises its contempt for those incapable of making that distinction." By way of elaborating on that, Geer says fairness "is a universal longing among both believers and non-believers; even the Marxist longs for it when he says, 'To each according to his need' even though he backs it with, 'From each according to his ability' enforced by a state without a God." Geer adds: "To be truly capable of fairness that is not mere mercy and certainly not procedural correctness, you must hear Kipling's words, 'To trust when all men doubt you, but make allowance for their doubting too.' Fairness takes no concern for whether in being fair you will be liked; indeed if you are driven by a desire to be liked, fairness will elude you."

BEING GOOD IN BUSINESS

As long as we are bordering on the poetic, I will insert here words from a poet friend, Samuel Hazo, who runs the International Poetry Forum in Pittsburgh, and with whom I discussed this project. He offered an interesting approach to the meaning of "being good" in business or along any other avenue of life. The poem is called "Scientia Non Est Virtus," and here are the relevant lines:

Old or young,
we learn too late that being
good is more than strict adherence
to commandments, laws or codes,
much more than being well
informed, and lightyears more
than all the learning in the world.
What is morality but shunning
   deeds we just can't do even
     when the opportunities present
     themselves?
      It's reflex
more than choice or reasoning. . . .
If that sounds like a substitute
for ignorance, then ignorance it is.
If it seems paradoxical
but vaguely possible, it's knowledge.
If it makes sense, it's wisdom.[3]

There is a practical wisdom associated with acting fairly and justly in business. Internalizing the right principles, as suggested earlier in this book, is the way one prepares to be reflexively just.

In the new corporate culture, some very old, often tried, but never true steps can lead the unsuspecting individual directly into the ethical swamp of personal injustice. The first step is taken when a person becomes enamored with "easy money." The second happens when one seeks the cover of "secrecy." The third step takes a person across the line or over the fence that was put in place by personal conscience. This fence has a sign posted on it that says: "Never violate a trust." Secrecy, easy money, and the violation of trust are, in combination, very dangerous to anyone's ethical health.

The degrees of engagement with this lethal combination (call it graft or corruption) can be measured in three categories, each representing money or something of significant monetary value: gift, bribe, extortion. Gifts are easily understood; what often is not understood is the inappropriateness of some gifts in workplace settings (private sector or public). Inappropriate gifts corrupt workplace relationships.

Bribery also corrupts. Bribery is always a secret arrangement. It has one party pay money or give something of value to another for neglecting a duty or performing some other dishonest act. Neglect of duty is the moral issue; in any instance of bribery, personal honor is up for sale. Not only is integrity violated, but injustice inevitably results because unfair gains are being taken and services that unknowing others have a right to expect are not delivered.

The third degree of corruption—extortion—is simply a hold-up. In a corrupt corporate culture, unjust payments are demanded if goods or services are to move in the market. Access to jobs is sometimes blocked by an outstretched palm waiting for a payoff. In times of economic ambiguity and uncertainty, the appeal of easy money will always be strong. A strong sense of justice will safeguard a person of integrity from violating any trust. If no trusts are violated, if no injustice is involved, a downsizing in response to economic necessity can be justified. But there is such a deep feeling of injustice, of unfair treatment, in so many downsized corners of our new corporate culture that those in control must examine their corporate conscience for evidence of injustice done to millions of separated employees in recent years. Those who feel the pressures of competition in this new corporate culture have to be very careful not to go the way of secrecy, in pursuit of easy money, at the price of a violated trust.

But most of the time fairness issues will emerge in far less dramatic form. There will be countless special situations peculiar to particular businesses or professions. Here is an example with which executive search consultants are quite familiar; and in this particular case, it came up as a hypothetical in the engagement interview where several top search firms were being considered by the directors of a major corporation, with the hope of winning the assignment to help that organization find its next chief executive officer.

FAIRNESS IN EXECUTIVE SEARCH

Search firms have an ethical prohibition against approaching any executive they had previously placed in a position to talk to them about moving again into a new job. Your client is the organization, not the person placed, in the executive search business. In fairness to your past client, you may not raid a company you had previously served to take away an executive you had previously placed and present that person as a candidate to a new client.

In the actual case I have in mind, the top outside director of the client company asked the headhunter in the engagement interview about a prominent CEO in another industry. "I can't touch him," the search consultant replied; "we put him in there." "Well, what if we made the contact," said the director, "and then delivered him to you so that you could do your work and present him along with a few others to us?" "Sorry, just can't do it," said the consultant; "it would violate our professional and ethical principles."

In a separate interview, the same director posed the same question to another search executive whose firm had placed another top manager who might be a good candidate for the job under consideration. "We put him in there and we're not supposed to go back," said the head of the search firm. "Well, suppose we talk to him and dig him up for you," said the outside director; "could you handle that?" "Yes, I suppose we could work around that," said the interviewee. That answer lost the engagement for him.

The successful applicant for the search assignment told me that when he got the assignment, the top outside director told him that he won it because of his stand on the ethical principle. And when the specifications were drawn up for the search, "integrity" was moved up from second place to first in the list of qualities needed in the executive to be chosen by the board. Needless to say, there had been a few integrity and reputational problems with the outgoing CEO, and the board wanted to find a successor who took integrity seriously.

The search firm that won this engagement had a potential problem of its own that one of their top executives had to nip in the bud. It happened that someone they had placed expressed an interest in a career change by moving into executive search. "You have all the qualities we like, but we can't touch you," was the immediate reply; "you're with a client, so it's hands off for us." A colleague in the search firm suggested to his boss, "Why don't you tell him to resign and that when he resigns we'll hire him. It works, and we won't get caught." That was not what the boss wanted to hear, and he took steps to make sure he did not hear it again.

Voices from the day-to-day, down-to-earth world of business tend to speak of justice in contractual, one-on-one or organization-to-organization terms. That is understandable because that is where most of the fairness issues arise to confront individuals in business. But justice moves from one-on-one commutative (or "exchange") justice, out to legal justice (staying within the law, which is there to serve the common good), and on to distributive justice (dealing with claims individuals or groups have to public goods), as well as social justice (which looks to all members of a group, hopes for a group initiative, and expects a group response to a genuine need).

Concern about micro-ethical issues is no indication that individualism reigns in business, and there is no interest there in macro-ethical or social concerns. We shall be meeting these wider issues in subsequent chapters dealing with corporate social responsibility and also with promotion and protection of the common good.

SEEK ADVICE AND COUNSEL

Steve Dymowski, a young vice president at the credit-card giant MBNA, told me that he found that he needed more than written policies to assure his fairness in managing people. In situations that appeared to require him "to make decisions outside of the policies," he followed a firm principle "never to act alone." "Seeking the advice and counsel of experienced personnel and senior managers is important in making sure that my decisions are fair and within reason. So I'd advise any manager to build a network of people that you trust to help you make the right decision." This idea will emerge again in Chapter 7 when we consider the way the principle of participation can shore up ethical decision making in large corporations.

I asked Michael Glezar, one of my MBA students who held a full-time job as a cost analyst with a construction company, to write a letter to himself upon completion of his MBA to get a preview of how he would negotiate the ethical landscape out there in front of him. He began by making the excellent point that "ethically speaking, for any manager or leader, it is critical that you not only do the right thing, but also be the right person." This is important. Being the right person, a person of character, points you in the right direction to meet the demands of justice.

In reflecting on his own integrity, Glezar reminded himself that

> About a year ago, you were securing long-term financing deals for a development venture for your company. There were three main parties involved: the banks, the nonprofit client, and your organization. One bank had offered you a very low interest rate, which would maximize the return to your company, yet had the most comprehensive set of obligations and highest expenses for the client (the nonprofit). You had to decide between maximizing the return to your company at the expense of the nonprofit, or making less while providing the client with a better deal. You decided in favor of the client. You did the right thing, but I think it took you a bit too long to decide. Having integrity translates into never having to think about what to do in a situation like this; you should internally already know.

Turning specifically to fairness, he noted in his letter to himself:

> People can and do notice if you favor certain people over others. A prime example of this happened about a month ago when you were tasked with promoting one of three subordinates. Problem number one was that your other subordinates weren't even to be considered. The second problem was that you and one of the three approved candidates were good friends. In the end, it was decided at a higher level to give the position to a new hire. Although that was not your decision, it represented the easy way out of the situation; it also gave you something to think about. Had you not shown a slight bias toward your friend, there would have been less stress. "Justice is blind"; so is fairness. You'll have to remember that if you are going to be fair in business to friends, or strangers you never met before.

A Pennsylvania lawyer with many business clients showed interest in this project, but he asked that I not use his name in relating his experience in the civil rights movement more than forty years earlier, an experience that remains influential in his dealing with clients to the present day. He volunteered as a young lawyer to advance civil rights in the not-yet-racially-desegregated South. Returning to his northern home city, where racism was not apparent but by no means nonexistent, he volunteered to speak to community, civic, and church groups about his experiences in the South. He shared with me two anecdotes that disillusioned, but did not discourage him then; and he did so to make the point that his vicarious experience with injustice in racial matters when he was young served to fire him with enthusiasm for the pursuit and promotion of justice throughout a long career of representing clients in business and countless other situations that had nothing to do with race.

Returning home from his advocacy work for civil rights in the 1960s, he told me:

> I realized that my most meaningful contribution then would be to tell that story to my local community. I sought after and welcomed speaking engagements to all groups, including service organization, educational, and religious institutions. In one particular instance I spoke to a service organization of my own Jewish faith community. I related what I had seen and heard and done; I encouraged others to become vigorous advocates for equality in every sense. It was probably my most heart-moving presentation to what I presumed to be a sympathetic and supportive group. I really spilled my guts.
>
> Imagine how I felt at the end of the talk when the first questioner said, "I have a rental property and a black man came to rent the apartment. I checked him out and he was fine, but I decided not to rent him the property." Then, to my amazement and after more than a half hour of what I thought was my powerful presentation on the relevance and importance of the struggle for equality, he asked, "I did the right thing, didn't I?" After that, I had no illusions about how steep the uphill slope was going to be for me in trying to represent the interests of the poor and powerless in my own home town.

On another occasion, my lawyer friend was visited, he told me, by an associate minister of a large Christian congregation who was trying to assist a black man trying to rent suitable living quarters. The minister accompanied the man on several unsuccessful attempts to rent an apartment. He spoke about this to his senior minister who told him, "If our church has to burn, we'll fight for this man's rights."

With this encouragement, the associate minister approached a property owner who was a member and generous supporter of his church and asked for help. The owner expressed an immediate willingness to help but then hesitated and asked,

"Is he black?" When he got his answer, he tried to withdraw, but the associate minister prevailed on him to rent the property and he did. Sometime later, for no apparent reason, the landlord told the black tenant that he would have to leave; if he chose not to, he would have to do janitorial and maintenance work on the properties as a condition of remaining there.

The associate minister consulted this same lawyer to see if the black man had a case on discrimination grounds. As my lawyer friend remembers:

> I said absolutely, provided you are a witness and are willing to sign an affidavit relating what you just told me. When he hesitated, I reminded him that when he went up into the pulpit the next Sunday, his sermon would be meaningless if he was not willing to follow through on this. He said he needed a day to think about whether he was ready to become a participant in a court proceeding. The next day he returned and told me that he would participate, but that his senior minister was no longer prepared to support civil rights and had said to him, "now you're on your own." The associate minister did give me an affidavit. We filed an action in federal court, and we prevailed. But I've never forgotten the cowardice and erosion of principle that I witnessed in this case.

TO BE FAIR IS TO RECOGNIZE THE BASIC VALUE OF ALL HUMANS

Louis Giraudo is a San Francisco lawyer with extensive business experience (chairman and CEO of Pacific Coast Baking Company). He told me that his approach to fairness is to "simply understand that one human being is not better than another human being. I may be a better lawyer, but not a better human being. So, in my view, to be fair is to recognize the basic value of all humans." This conviction has shaped his outlook in all situations of his business and professional life. He does mergers and acquisitions and is known as a "transactional counsel." By his own account, his success with and for clients is not unrelated to his awareness that there is equal human value represented in the persons on either side of any transaction.

Grounded emotionally and intellectually in this kind of an approach to fairness, Lou Giraudo had these words of advice for one of his sons just starting out in investment banking:

> You've arrived and things are already in motion. You'll encounter in others a sense of entitlement that has settled in and you'll see and experience competitive dishonesty. Stay above it and know that your family, faith, and friends are with you. You need not mark your success or failure by how much money you make, but rather by how much good your efforts are creating. Don't cheat. Don't lie. Don't steal. Leave all of that to those who have no life. When they finish, they inevitably look at the bank account and they'll find themselves asking: Is that all there is? Where's my family? Where is real friendship? The bank account is full but life is empty.

"I find myself becoming more and more cynical," Giraudo said to me. "Too often I see friends, acquaintances, and enemies putting the quest for the dollar above all else. Too often I see these same people pursuing a path of borderline business practice. The accumulation of wealth has become for many, I'm sorry to say, the only benchmark of success. They achieve their goals at the price of unethical and illegal activity."

"Some say that life is a lottery," Giraudo continued. "That may be true to some extent, but you are making choices even when you pick the numbers. An honest banker can make lots of money. An honest and happy banker is the one who makes it work not only for himself, but also for the common good. He's a person who makes the right choices for the right reasons. That's what I want for my son. I tell him that we make our own luck and choose our own numbers."

Steve Harlan, retired vice chairman of KPMG, has an interesting approach to fairness. With an accountant's characteristic discretion, he did not name names when he told me, "There are many business leaders who by all appearances are successful and who, in my judgment, are not fair. They play favorites. Something usually happens in the long run to these people—sort of payback time." The long run had already caught up with some of them; their names were in the headlines. Others, Harlan believes, will be caught by that long-run lasso in due time.

Sister Mary Kelly, a healthcare administrator whose wise letter to a young manager appears in Chapter 13, would agree with Harlan's emphasis on playing favorites in analyzing fairness in the workplace. She looks for "evenness and consistency, unhampered by subjective factors."

Ed Petrie, owner of a small residential and commercial mortgage company, describes his industry as "fraught with violations of rules and regulations." He would agree with Harlan's view that justice will be served in the long run. "The companies that play by the rules sometimes find themselves losing out to unethical companies. However, the practices and standards exhibited by those 'cheating' companies always seem to boomerang and return with a vengeance. Their people are convicted of fraud and they suffer both bad publicity and loss of revenue." Ethical firms do not have to worry about that. He pointed out that an uneven advantage is not necessarily an unfair advantage, so it is not unjust, he told me, when his experience and creativity outpoint his competitor's inertia.

A useful image to append to this consideration of justice as fairness is the one mentioned earlier, the familiar scales of justice, the two trays in balance on a scale. You see this symbol on courthouse walls and in law offices. It belongs in the mind of anyone in business, functioning as a framework through which to view the world of business decision making and the gains and losses that are part of everyday business life.

Relating to another fairly in business does not mean that you cannot outpoint the other and win the game. It simply means that you have to play that game within the rules, never taking an unfair advantage at the expense of the other. You win your points within the rules on the playing field; you don't get them by stealing your opponent's numbers from the scoreboard and posting them under your name.

CHAPTER SIX

Human Dignity

In any workplace anywhere, you will find persons across the full range of employment responsibility—top to bottom in rank, newcomer or veteran in seniority—who share a common human longing. They want to be respected as persons; they want to be treated with dignity; they want to find meaning in their lives and work.

As I indicated earlier, the principle of human dignity is the bedrock principle of both personal and social ethics. In the new corporate culture, human dignity is taking a beating. In the context of corporate downsizing, for example, workers at all levels are being treated as if they were disposable parts. In many cases, bottom lines and balance sheets get more attention than human beings (too often regarded as human doings) who lose their jobs to "re-engineered" processes or to "reinvention" in the workplace. Involuntary separation from employment will be inevitable for many, so the ethical question is how each unique human person is to be laid off. It must be done with dignity and a modicum of security—severance pay, extended healthcare insurance, retraining or relocation assistance. Although employees will, regrettably, but for sound economic reasons, continue to be separated from their jobs, they must never be viewed by those making the downsizing decisions as disposable parts.

With the Enron debacle came the shocking revelations that executives enriched themselves by exercising stock options, based on insider knowledge, while employees were left holding empty 401-K bags that had been loaded with now worthless Enron stock. Their human rights, as well as their human dignity, were violated by greedy executives.

Sexual harassment in the workplace makes the headlines with troubling regularity. It would not happen if the principle of human dignity became part of the attitude and outlook of all who interact with one another in the same place of employment. This principle draws a defensive ring around the human person who, on or off the job, is never an object. He or she is always the subject of rights, entitled to respect simply for being human.

As I was writing this, I decided on a whim just to type "principle of human dignity" into the Google search engine and see what came up. I arrived immediately at the Web site of Ascension Health Care (http://www.ascensionhealth.org), the nation's largest Catholic and largest not-for-profit healthcare system. Its network of hospitals and related health facilities spreads over twenty states and the District of Columbia, employing 100,000 people. By a strange coincidence, I was scheduled to speak on the subject of organizational ethics to trustees and managers of the Nashville, Tennessee, affiliates of this system within two weeks of making my random Internet contact.

For the moment, let me simply give the reader what is available there on the Web site, where the principle of human dignity is described as "the intrinsic worth that inheres in every human being." The statement goes on to explain that from the Catholic/Christian perspective "the source of human dignity is rooted in the concept of *Imago Dei*, in Christ's redemption and in our ultimate destiny of union with God."

The *Imago Dei* reference has a theological history alluded to by biblical scholar John R. Donahue, S.J., when he notes that in its original significance the "image of God" did

> not mean some human quality (intellect or free will) or the possession of "sanctifying grace." Two interpretations enjoy some exegetical support today. One view is

that, just as ancient Near Eastern kings erected "images" of themselves in subject territory, so humans are God's representatives, to be given the same honor due God. Claus Westermann argues that the phrase means that humans were created to be God's counterpart, creatures analogous to God with whom God can speak and who will hear God's word. . . . In either of these interpretations, all men and women prior to identification by race, social status, religion, or sex are worthy of respect and reverence.[1]

Donahue explains further that, "Men and women are God's representatives and conservation partners in the world, with a fundamental dignity that must be respected and fostered. They are to exist in independence and mutual support and are to care for the world with respect, as for a gift received from God."[2]

Walter J. Burghardt, S.J., who cites these excerpts from Donahue in his book *Justice: A Global Adventure*, writes that human dignity is "rooted in the image and reflection of God in each human person, an imaging of God that can be defaced but never obliterated. From that unique dignity, flow significant rights. Not only the right to life but related rights necessary for each one's integral development as a person: for example, the right to a job, to a living wage, to decent housing, to education, to healthcare, to respect."[3] Intellect and free will set us apart from lower forms of life; they contribute to our "imaging" God in the world, but there is more to it than that. As the example of ancient Near East emperors making sure their images were prominently placed in subject territories suggests, any man or woman, to the eye of the believer, reflects the presence of God in the world. Even the nonbeliever can recognize that a human person possessed of intellect and will stands apart from the rest of nature and is therefore all the more worthy of respect.

Of course, we all know that some persons act as if they were God in the workplace—"lording it over" others, exercising "omniscience," always occupying the "judgment seat." Reminding them of their proper place is neither to assault nor insult their dignity; it is simply an invitation for them to get real. The reference above to those kings from the ancient Near East making sure that images of themselves appeared in territories over which they reigned might lead some to recall seeing the picture of a president, whom we may not have admired, in every federal building, or the photograph of an unpopular prelate in every rectory. Yet there is something attractive and appealing to us humans who want our dignity to be acknowledged and respected, to think of ourselves as bearing the "image of God" in the humble, or even not-so-humble settings of our workplace surroundings.

AN INCLUSIVE DECISION-MAKING PROCESS

Ascension Health, by the way, has an "Organizational Ethics Discernment Process" outlined in a small leaflet that is put in the hands of every employee. The seven-step process, to be followed in practical decision-making situations, follows:

(1) "Identify the Central Question" and note how this particular decision impacts the organization;

(2) "Consider Subsidiarity," which means placing the decision point at the appropriate level surrounded by the relevant expertise;

(3) "Identify the Relevant Facts," including identification of applicable regulations, policies, professional standards, and possible outcomes;

(4) "Identify Salient Moral Concerns" relating to human dignity, the common good, justice, fairness, stewardship, and human rights;

(5) "Consider Alternatives," noting what other organizations do or do not do in similar situations;

(6) "Decide & Justify," which prompts a consideration of whether the directly intended effects and the chosen means are consistent with relevant moral norms and Ascension Health's values;

(7) Follow-Up & Review," which includes consideration of what might be done differently next time.

The whole process turns on respect for the human dignity of those who make and will be affected by the decision.

Not all organizations will have this kind of seven-step security, but most organizations have the potential to produce a good process if they simply listen to experienced and principled persons who work there every day. Here are a few voices from the workplace on this question of human dignity.

"Recognition is the key word," says veteran consultant John Thomas. "We all want to think that we are important. Just saying 'thank you' is a very positive motivator and helps a person's self-esteem. Besides, when a worker knows that he or she has the respect of a peer, or the boss, it is much easier to motivate that person to overcome any shortcomings that need attention." He then went on to tell me a couple of stories. The first dated back to his work in the 1980s with First Wisconsin, a bank holding company in Milwaukee. The real-estate loan portfolio was in trouble; there were rumors that the bank might fail. A key executive was charged with the responsibility of turning things around. When John Thomas met him, let's call him Gilbert, it was his first day in a new office. Thomas was surprised to see that his desk was stacked with $100 bills. This was their first meeting, and the client told the consultant that their meeting would be delayed a bit because he had to talk first with his employees. Gilbert invited Thomas to come along, and this is what John Thomas observed:

> He picked up the stack of bills and went out and handed one to each employee, thanking each and asking them for support. He did some jaw-boning with some about this loan or that and listened to their ideas. I spent the whole afternoon watching this and saw the positive impact it was having on the personnel.
>
> Gilbert energized what had been a heavily criticized and demoralized department. They responded to him.

Eventually, they got the problems solved, and Gilbert went on to become the bank's CEO. He treated everyone equally; he listened to their ideas, and they responded to his direction.

Another anecdote recounted by John Thomas goes back to his early days in business with Johnson & Johnson in Chicago.

We had a minor problem with product quality that could only be solved by the workers paying more attention as the product came off the machines. Each worker was scored daily on the quality of his or her production. We knew that a modest two-to-three percent improvement in the scores would make the problem disappear. We also knew that a small increase in production quality could mean a boost in both volume and revenue.

So, we created a quality-improvement contest for our eighty production workers with the prize of a vacation for two in San Francisco. We gave it a corny name like "The Gold Rush of 1965," if I remember correctly. Workers could earn "miles" when their daily quality scores exceeded the target, and the first one with enough miles to reach San Francisco would be the winner. Before announcing the contest, we painted a huge map of the U.S.A. on one of the walls; it highlighted the path from Chicago to San Francisco. As a build-up to this "great" program, we waited a week before telling the workers what the map was all about. Well, that was the plan.

It went over like a lead balloon. The union stewards were outraged that we dare to recognize one person over another. Some of the male machine operators said it was a plan for "sissies." I was crushed by the rejection, but my wiser and older boss said, "Let's give this a couple of days, I think it will work."

The very next day, Mary, one of our first-shift packers, got a perfect score on her production. We put Mary's name up on the map somewhere near the Iowa-Illinois border. Everyone saw it; the ridicule stopped, and the race was on. We introduced small prizes at 200-mile intervals, so someone was being recognized every day. At the end, we gave away two free trips, and I gained a valuable bond with my crew.

Years later, one of my consulting specialties was the development of incentive compensation programs. Incentives, of course, are attempts to change human behavior. I learned from the map-and-miles experiment that recognition is a big part of this and that it often accomplishes a result that outstrips the monetary award.

GOOD PROFESSIONAL CONDUCT

Joe Kraemer takes a pragmatic, rather than a philosophical or theological approach to this question. "I make it a point," he says, "to be sensitive when dealing with support personnel. While this is good professional conduct, it also pays dividends in that sooner or later I will need an extraordinary effort from the support staff. If I treated them in any way other than with dignity, they would not have been there for me." Fair enough, you might say, and you will be right. You get an echo here, and see a good secular application of the Golden Rule, which, of course, shows great respect for human dignity.

Ralph Lancaster's approach elaborates on Joe Kraemer's understanding of the principle of human dignity. Lancaster sees it as "double-faceted." One's "carriage and activities" display dignity or its absence, he says, so "if dignity is possessed, the possessor is deemed worthy of the respect and esteem that fellow human beings show in return." But given human frailties, he concludes, "dignity is likely to come across as somewhat stuffy" and won't be permanently maintained. He is not denying the intrinsic worth of another person, just acknowledging the frailty of the one who must pay to that other person constant respect.

This judicious man was beginning, at this point in our exchange, to show some signs of pessimism. "Today's climate of greed and selfishness has so permeated at least the larger corporate world, that all these values and principles we're talking about have been deliberately blurred and undermined." He went on to say, "It is all about money and power, not necessarily in that order. Whether it's Hollywood, TV, sports, politics or business, the bedrock values, formerly so important to our culture, have been eroded to the point of near irrelevance." Then he tipped his hand by indicating that his pessimistic eye was on the next generation: "I believe that the average American still subscribes to these values but that, little by little, our youth are being taught that these values are unimportant and are actually impediments to success."

That got me wondering if, given the tsunami-like force of adolescent peer pressure, whether it might be more accurate to say that our youth are teaching themselves, and the elders are letting them down by leading value-vacant lives or, perhaps more accurately, by failing to post high enough for all to see the solid values that still have a good chance of being caught by the young.

Jim Leeper caught all of the "right stuff" from his father many years ago. I was impressed with his reaction to my questions about having the right values and principles in business. He is president and CEO of the Pittsburgh-based Louis F. Leeper Company, which provides sales and marketing services to manufacturers of consumer packaged goods sold generally through grocery, drug, and mass-merchandising stores. Given Ralph Lancaster's doubts about the next generation, I was impressed, first, by Jim's admiration and imitation of his father's (Louis Leeper, founder of the company) business principles and, second, by the following goal stated in the company's current mission statement: "Teach the next generation, through our actions, how to succeed through service to others and how to prosper by doing the right thing." I will let Jim Leeper tell the story in his own words, which he wrote to me after our original conversation.

I had an enlightening conversation with my Dad shortly after I finished graduate school (the University of Pittsburgh's school of public and international affairs). Despite my education, I was confused about my future. My Dad for some reason felt strongly that I was tailor-made to run the business he started in 1959. I have four siblings, all a lot smarter and talented than I. Why my Dad did not try to persuade any of them to enter the business, I'll never understand.

The conversation was brief. Dad asked me what I wanted to do for a living. I told him I did not know, but I wanted to work to do something good for others. I wish I could say my motive was altruistic, but that would not be entirely true. I was motivated, in part, by ignorance, an ignorance born from years of a subtle bias that certain jobs (any profit-making activity) are for those who worry only about themselves, while other jobs (teaching, non-profit sector) are for those who care for others more than themselves. One was noble; the other ignoble. I was vainly concerned that people would view me as the latter were I to pursue a career in the private sector.

I was too foolish to recognize that my Dad, who along with my Mom, was the least self-centered person I ever knew, chose the private sector and was at complete peace with himself. How could this be?

My Dad answered the question when he said something like this. "Listen, Jim, there are lots of ways to help people, but one of the best is to give someone a job. Not just any job, but a great job, a job that pays well for working hard, that includes medical benefits to help people protect their family, that provides the kind of atmosphere that people love so they can love their jobs, that maintains the right perspective that keeps faith and family first."

My Dad got what a lot of others in and out of business never will. He knew that God calls each of us to serve others in different ways—some to teach, some to preach, some to provide jobs, some to provide resources, some just to work to make an honest living and support their families. All of those people have dignity and so do all those ways of making a living. The important thing is to serve others not yourself. If you prosper in doing so, so much the better; you now have more resources to share with others. The nobility is in the service, not the profession.

AN EXCEPTIONAL WORKING ATMOSPHERE

On the question of following the principle of human dignity in the workplace, Jim Leeper points to this provision in the firm's mission statement: "Provide an exceptional working atmosphere for our associates, one that offers challenging jobs with reasonable workloads, excellent support systems, a sufficient number of qualified associates to share the load, leaders who serve and a perspective that places faith and family first." Obviously, this acorn fell not far from the tree; the notion that human dignity can be served through the provision of good employment opportunities is alive and well at the company founded by his father.

Dan Altobello was chairman, president, and CEO of Caterair International Corporation. I asked him about his views relative to human dignity, and he replied that he simply presupposes it in relationships with employees. His experience prompted him to "assume that everyone wants to do a good job. Let only their actions prove this false. Praise in public; condemn in private. Make everyone feel proud."

Chairman Jack Conroy, of Investment Properties Corporation, took a reflective, philosophical approach to all the questions I asked him. On this question of human dignity, he commented that your perception of another's worth is usually something that occurs "subtly, not overtly." Respect for another's dignity should be "an underlying assumption that must be arrived at intellectually and incorporated into one's moral system. The logical consequence of the denial of this principle is the Holocaust." He thinks that even an "inadvertent expression of an attitude that subverts the principle that everyone has inherent worth will be the destruction of the possibility of a long-term business relationship." And he notes that "this is especially important in dealing with persons who differ from me in terms of religion, gender, race, age, or sexual orientation."

Some executives like Barry LeBlanc, president and CEO of Pamlab, a pharmaceutical company in Mandeville, Louisiana, tend to think of human dignity mainly as "an HR [Human Resources] issue. In my case," he told me, "I stress for our company to care for a person regardless of position or prominence in the organization. We all have feelings, we all have problems, and we all hope to succeed. Regardless of their contribution to the bottom line, everyone here has value to our company." He thinks that being president of a privately held company makes it easier to uphold both the outlook and the principle presented here. Not all would agree with LeBlanc's conviction that an employer's respect for the dignity of workplace associates should open him or her up to "discussing personal issues with employees and being prepared to help solve those personal issues." Some would take the opposite view that respect for your employees' dignity should prompt employers to respect their privacy, and even if they raise the problems, solutions to those problems should be the work of others, not the boss.

HE WHO TALKS TO THE JANITOR UNDERSTANDS THE ORGANIZATION

I know of a professor in an elite business school who uses an unusual device to make his students more aware of the importance of recognizing the dignity of all persons in the workplace. In his mid-term exam, he asks: "Please list the name of the person who cleans this classroom every day." In response to the howls of protest and charges of unfairness that question always generates, he simply says:

Not unfair, because I'm telling you now that I will make it up to you by asking the same question on the final. You now have that question in advance of the test. And, by the way, if you don't have enough sensitivity to recognize that a real person with a real name works for you every day by putting this place into good shape for class, then you're going to fail as a boss in the real world of work by not noticing that you have real people with real dignity on your payroll who happen to be doing important but menial jobs.

When I told this story to my MBA students at Loyola College during the Spring 2005 semester, one of them commented that her father had impressed upon her the wisdom of this saying: "He who talks to the janitor understands the organization." That pleasantly pragmatic view stands in contrast (but not opposition) to a theological perspective provided by Miami University of Ohio management professor and author Charles Watson who, in discussing human dignity, said to me: "Everyone, as a creature of God, is God's own. So how we treat others—what we do to and for other humans—reveals our respect for God."

Adobe co-founder Chuck Geschke's awareness that his business is built with intellectual capital makes it easy for him to acknowledge the importance of the principle of human dignity. As I reported in Chapter 4, Geschke says Adobe's strength is not based on assets like factories, warehouses, storefronts, or mining and mineral rights. Adobe's capital is its principled, highly educated, and well-trained people. So, in his view, it is the behavior, commitment, and cooperation of the people— the culture they create—that makes the financial success of the business possible. To translate his conviction that respect for human dignity runs from top to bottom and back to the top in his organization, Geschke says: "At Adobe, everyone sweeps the floor."

Cynthia Danaher, retired vice president of Hewlett-Packard, says that "every person counts" is her take on human dignity.

For her, this principle carries over into the principle of participation, which is a practical acknowledgment of the conviction that "each person matters." This makes practical good sense too, she says, because "decisions made by many are bought into faster."

Paul Montrone, Chairman and CEO of Fisher Scientific Instrumental Inc., has an interesting approach to the principle of human dignity. "This is where we are all equal," he says, "at this most basic level; but above this level you move into fairness." And his take on fairness stems from a conviction that "treating equals equally" is an inadequate description of justice because, in his view, "there are no 'equals'—we are all unique and must be treated as such, for good or bad; some are promoted, some get fired. Treating inequals inequally might be a better way of saying it."

The point he makes is one worth remembering, namely, that each person is simply unique. Period. Unique means exactly what it says—one and only. It is an imprecise use of language to speak of something or someone being "somewhat," "more," "less," or "most" unique. Unique means unicity. It points to the unrepeatable onceness of a human life, to the altogether special identity and existence of every human person. An appreciation of this understanding of uniqueness will prevent the one who possesses it from ever considering another person as "just one more," a phrase that novelist Alice McDermott puts in the mind of one of her characters whose son, in this disappointed mother's opinion, is going nowhere ("on a slow march to an unremarkable end") at the beginning of his business career:

> She'd be in the kitchen when Dennis came down in the morning, making his coffee and buttering his toast, but she'd never eat anything herself. . . . Instead, she'd lean against the counter and watch her son, assessing: the cut of his suit, the knot in his tie, the prospects for his future. Although at that time in her life she had held only two jobs herself—one in a bakery in Brooklyn, one in the

mailroom of the gas company—she had a considered opinion about what the workaday world could do to you, and it wasn't a very high opinion, either, despite her Protestant blood.

In part, she objected to the monotony of nine-to-five, the tedium, the hours and days you ended up wishing away, swinging from one Saturday morning to another like a monkey at the zoo. In part, it was the anonymity. . . . Once you boarded the subway or the bus or joined the crawling stream of automobiles or found your space in the revolving door, the elevator, behind the desk or the counter or the machine, you became what you really were—you became, when you got right down to it, what you really were: one of the so many million, just one more.[4]

The principle of human dignity can serve both as a window through which you can look at others in the workplace and as a mirror in which you can view yourself. Either way, what you see is unique. In function of their uniqueness, the persons who populate any given workplace can make that place, and all that happens there, special, challenging, one of a kind. It all depends on their point of view.

———————

Select your own favorite piece of sculpture to serve as an image of human dignity. The Statue of Liberty might work for some; Michelangelo's "David" for others. George Segal's sculpted figures representing five broken men standing in a bread line during the Great Depression enhance the FDR Memorial in Washington, DC; they might also serve to point to an enduring human dignity that could not be broken by hunger and poverty. Think of any good sculpture you have seen and select one great figure as a mental keepsake to remind you of the dignity of the human person.

CHAPTER SEVEN

Workplace Participation

Every human person in any workplace has a right to have some say in the decisions that affect his or her livelihood. To be shut out of all discussion is to be denied respect for one's human dignity. Workplace participation is not unrelated to the corporate culture and the attitude of top management. The late Al Casey, whose career put him in a number of impressive executive positions, including the chairmanship of American Airlines, used to say, "you have to walk the halls and introduce yourself," whenever you move into the corner office. He wanted others to know that, as their new CEO, his "first assignment is to become part of a team, not its leader." His advice to himself: "Listen, listen, listen. If your mouth is open, you are not learning."[1]

Al Casey invited his friend and college classmate Jack Valenti to write the foreword to his memoir, *Casey's Law,* which has a subtitle that spells out the law: "If Something Can Go Right, It Should." This, of course, is the optimistic opposite to the famous Murphy's Law ("If anything can go wrong, it will"); it says a lot about Casey's approach to management. In the foreword, Valenti writes that Casey "is a man who understands the basic frame of the human condition, for he honors the individual dignity of those working under him and treats them with a warm affection that is both unfeigned and unpretentious." Valenti continues:

> Put another way, there are countless men and women
> who can dissect a financial document, who are artisans

of the spreadsheet and architects of shareholder enhancement, who can organize, and administer, and "do" board meetings. But there are too few CEOs who can walk the factory floor or the office corridors and achieve genuine rapport with the men and women who work there, earning their respect and inspiring their pride and loyalty. Casey can.

Before meeting more managers and examining their commitment to participation, let's go back for a moment to the downsizing decision that in the late 1980s became a prominent feature of the new corporate culture. The ethical thing to do in this new and evolving corporate culture is, in anticipation of layoff, to involve the employee in planning and in the execution of the plan. This means preparation for separation should that have to happen. If participation is a way of workplace life, it will extend skill-training opportunities not just for those about to leave, but for those who will stay. The "value added" potential and the productivity of employees who will remain is enhanced by their fullest possible participation in the business of the business. You will hear more on everyday, across-the-organization participation later in this chapter. For now, consider participation on the governing board.

Participation moves from top to bottom, bottom to top, and all across the organization. Governance guides the operation; management executes. Under the broad canopy of the principle of participation, those up there at the very top are the board members. The search for "tone at the top" has to reach higher than top management; it has to look to the board of directors. Some notable failures to participate at this level are part of the sad story of corporate wrongdoing and collapse in the earliest years of the present century.

Governance is, by definition, participation. Not to participate is not to meet the responsibilities of governance. As I shall explain more fully shortly, ethical analysis of governance failures often reveals an absence of courage. Speaking of board responsibility, a lawyer friend remarked to me, "You never want to be in a position where you would have to admit that the question occurred to you, but you just didn't ask it."

I recommend Bill George's book *Authentic Leadership*[2] to anyone interested in getting caught up on the preventive role good governance can play in avoiding corporate scandals. The author is former chairman and CEO of Medtronic. His title selection for his fifteenth chapter says it all: "Governance Is Governance." Do not talk about it; do it. Participate in governance, and the job will get done. George takes the reader inside the boardroom and describes how "good governance lies in the chemistry between the board and the CEO."[3] Wait a minute, I hear the reader saying, isn't that the problem— cozy chemistry? It could be, but the right chemistry means awareness on the CEO's part that the board is in charge, and right chemistry fosters both comfort and courage at the board level to raise any question, to request any report, and not to be intimidated by the powerful personalities of top managers.

PARTICIPATION AS AN EXERCISE IN INDEPENDENCE

Although a clique of outside directors can bond too closely with a strong-willed CEO (if they happen to constitute the executive compensation committee, as is often the case, the chemistry will surely be counterproductive), strong independent directors have to be ready to speak up, speak out, risk unpopularity in the board room, and, as one from the oil services industry said to me, "be ready to shoot that snake as soon as you spot it moving through the grass."

Outside, or independent, directors should meet alone from time to time. One of them should, if the CEO is also board chair, head up an independent governance committee and be designated as the board's "presiding director" with power to call and chair executive sessions held in the absence of management and other inside directors.

I think devices like these are necessary because I agree with a view expressed to me by veteran CPA John Coughlan, that "management, through the proxy process (so often under-utilized and passive), owns the board of directors, and through the board, it owns the outside accountant. Members of the board are well compensated," he said:

> They know their continued presence on the board and their prospects for serving on other boards depend on their willingness to go along. I read somewhere that Vernon Jordan, in addition to being a partner in a prestigious law firm, serves on eleven boards of directors. Meaningful service on a board requires at least 200 hours per year, so eleven boards would raise that requirement to at least 2,200 hours, leaving little time for an important law practice.

Coughlan wrapped up this reflection by saying, "In management's view, the 'good' directors are those that turn up for meetings, read the *Wall Street Journal*, and only pay attention when the chairperson calls for a vote. And if the chairperson pulls his or her right ear, they vote Yea, and if it's the left ear, Nay."

Former U.S. Attorney General Richard L. Thornburgh (who prefers, even in formal print, to be called Dick) served as court appointed examiner in the WorldCom Bankruptcy Proceedings. In December 2003, he gave his reflections on that experience in a speech at a dinner meeting of the Committee on Federal Regulation of Securities of the American Bar Association.[4] Thornburgh saw WorldCom as "a kind of poster child for corporate governance failures in this new century." There was, he said, "the failure of directors to recognize, and deal effectively with, abuses [that reflected] a 'culture of greed' within the corporation's top management. . . . The company overstated its income by approximately $11 billion, overstated its balance sheet by approximately $75 billion and, as a result, caused losses in shareholder value of as much as $250 billion." Thornburgh went on to say:

Our investigation concludes that WorldCom was dominated by Bernard Ebbers and Scott Sullivan, the former Chief Executive Officer and Chief Financial Officer of the Company, respectively, with virtually no checks or restraints placed on their actions by the Board of Directors or other management. Significantly, although many present or former officers and directors of WorldCom told us that they had misgivings at the time regarding decisions or actions by Mr. Ebbers or Mr. Sullivan during the relevant period, there is no evidence that any of these officers and directors made any attempts to curb, stop or challenge the conduct they deemed questionable and inappropriate. Instead . . . it appears that the Company's officers and directors went along with Mr. Ebbers and Mr. Sullivan, even under circumstances that suggested corporate actions were at best imprudent, and at worst inappropriate and fraudulent. . . .

In fact, several multi-billion dollar acquisitions were approved by the Board of Directors following discussions that lasted for 30 minutes or less and without the directors receiving a single piece of paper on the terms or implications of the transactions. . . .

Our investigation raised significant concerns regarding the circumstances surrounding the Company's loan of more than $400 million to Mr. Ebbers. As detailed in our reports, the Compensation and Stock Option Committee of the Board of Directors agreed to provide enormous loans and a separate guaranty for Mr. Ebbers without initially informing the full Board or taking appropriate steps to protect the company. Further, as the loans and guaranty increased, the Committee failed to perform appropriate due diligence that would have demonstrated that the collateral offered by Mr. Ebbers was grossly inadequate to support the company's extension of credit to him, in light of his substantial other loans and obligations. Our investigation reflected that the Board was similarly at fault for not raising any questions about the loans and merely adopting, without meaningful consideration, the recommendations of the Compensation Committee.

Not raising any questions? Without meaningful consideration? Those are minimum participation requirements for any board of directors.

Mr. Thornburgh concluded:

> Next only in importance to the absence of internal controls as a cause of this debacle was the lack of transparency between senior management and the Board of Directors at WorldCom. . . . I believe that this failing helped to foster an environment and culture that permitted the fraud to grow dramatically. A culture and internal processes that discourage or implicitly forbid scrutiny and detailed questioning are breeding grounds for fraudulent misdeeds. In tandem with the accounting irregularities, these shortcomings fostered the illusion that WorldCom was far more healthy and successful than it actually was during the relevant period. Ultimately, they also produced massive investor losses, bankruptcy for WorldCom, and a profound loss of confidence in our financial markets and economic system.

WorldCom's directors were, according to the court-appointed examiner, "all too often a passive rubber stamp for management and especially Mr. Ebbers."

Is it an exaggeration to say that all of this could have been avoided if the board had done its job? Perhaps. But it is no exaggeration to say, as Mr. Thornburgh did when he participated in a panel discussion on corporate governance in late 2004 at Georgetown University's Woodstock Theological Center, that "a culture that emphasizes ethical conduct will make more difference than all the laws and regulations promulgated by various government agencies." He acknowledged that the temptation is always there to view additional statutory and regulatory enactments as government-imposed impediments to smooth and efficient corporate governance, but he does not agree. "I think Sarbanes-Oxley and similar initiatives will empower the 'good guys,' and there are plenty of them out there in the business system, far more than the few bad apples that spoiled WorldCom and Enron."

I was on that panel with Governor Thornburgh at Georgetown; we were joined by Tom Saporito, who, as a consultant, specializes in board selection and corporate governance. After each of us had spoken, and before questions came from the audience, each of us was asked by the moderator to make a one-minute summary statement. We were meeting in the library of the Woodstock Theological Center; off to the side, but within clear view of the audience, was a bust of John Courtney Murray, the great Woodstock theologian who was the principal architect of the Second Vatican Council's famous document on religious freedom. As I looked at the sculpted head of Father Murray mounted nearby, I recalled that Walter Burghardt, his Jesuit colleague for many years at Woodstock, told me more than once that Murray used to say to him during difficult or stressful times, "Courage, Walter, it's far more important than intelligence!" I repeated that in my summary comment and underscored the importance of courage on the part of corporate directors if debacles like Enron and WorldCom are to be avoided in the future.

When asked which characteristics he most admired in other people, Karl Rahner, another great Jesuit theologian, said simply: "Decency, courage, cheerfulness, helpfulness, fidelity." When are all those qualities going to find their way into the job descriptions of corporate executives?

Although Dick Thornburgh mentioned almost in passing in his 2003 American Bar Association speech that liability for corporate directors "is still a developing field," and that "recent court decisions have already pointed to an expanded potential for directors' liability," neither he nor anyone else was ready to predict what actually happened on March 18, 2005. That was the day of final approval of a landmark agreement by 11 former independent directors of WorldCom to pay $20 million out of their own pockets to settle a civil suit representing hundreds of thousands of investors whose WorldCom holdings became worthless when the company went bankrupt in 2002. The investors succeeded in holding the directors accountable for mismanagement and fraud that happened under their watch. The settlement with the directors came in the same week that WorldCom's founder and CEO, Bernard J. Ebbers, was found guilty of directing the $11 billion accounting fraud that took the company down.

Governance, as I said earlier, is, by definition, participation. Not to participate is not to meet the responsibilities of governance. And I am convinced that ethical analysis of governance failures will often reveal an absence of courage. As I mentioned earlier in this chapter, a lawyer friend once remarked to me that, "You never want to be in a position where you would have to admit that the question occurred to you, but you just didn't ask it." He was talking, of course, about the absence of courage.

NEEDED: A CHIEF COURAGE OFFICER

PriceWaterhouseCoopers took out an ad in major newspapers in January 2005 to say that every corporation needs a "chief courage officer." Not a bad idea. It is not likely to happen, however, even though many corporations are appointing "chief ethics officers," and their portfolio will be carried more gracefully and effectively if the person bearing the title is a person of courage. I think courage has to be part of the corporate culture; it has to be a shared value. If courage is a dominant value helping to shape a corporate culture, an act of courage on the part of one individual will draw both a positive reaction and imitation from others in the organization.

Think of Enron's Ken Lay or WorldCom's Bernie Ebbers against the background of Robert Greenleaf's observation: "To be a lone chief atop a pyramid is *abnormal and corrupting*. . . . When someone is moved atop a pyramid, that person no longer has colleagues, only subordinates. Even the frankest and bravest of subordinates do not talk with their boss in that same way that they talk with colleagues who are equals, and normal communication patterns become warped."[5] A strong, participating—that is, fully informed, fully awake, outspoken and questioning—governing board is needed to correct that abnormality and prevent possible corruption. Greenleaf thinks that the title "chief executive officer," "and the single chief concept it conveys, should disappear as an anachronism."[6] It will come as no surprise that Greenleaf believes that "*no one, absolutely no one, is to be entrusted with the operational use of power without the close oversight of fully functioning trustees.*"[7]

Back now to the practicalities of participation in the workplace. Fred Gluck, who retired in 1994 as managing partner of McKinsey & Co., the world-famous consulting firm, saw the inner workings of countless business organizations. It is his view that "effective workplaces respect everyone's idea and needs, but do not necessarily include everyone in decision making. Some things in business, including participation, must be earned." That's a point to be borne in mind, but remember that once accepted as an operating principle within the organization—that is, as a prominent feature of the organization's culture—a commitment to participation will prompt management to include employees in the process of decision making that could affect them adversely. A good example would be the decision to outsource certain functions. Colleges and universities, for example, are increasingly turning to outsourcing as a way to improve efficiency and enhance revenue in activities like the bookstore, food services, and printing. "Outsourcing Can Make Sense, but Proceed With Caution" is the headline advice over an article on this topic in the *Chronicle of Higher Education.*[8] Author Paul Davis, drawing on his past experience as director of finance and auxiliary services at Duke University, advises: "Be straightforward with employees about outsourcing, and try to speak before the rumor mill speaks for you." [9]

Cutting rumors off at the pass makes for both lower blood pressure and higher productivity in the workplace. Speaking in advance of both rumors and actual decisions is good management practice. Because participation in this context applies to those who are likely to be affected adversely by an outsourcing decision—for example, bookstore clerks as well as managers, cafeteria workers, and veteran printers now on the university payroll—it is important that they have precise information on the options that might be taken and a voice in deciding which option is best for the organization overall. Then they will be informed participants in the next stage of decision making, namely, whether there is a continuation-of-employment opportunity for them with the new contractor, and, if not, whether some training to update and enhance skills, as well as outplacement services, will be available to them during the transition.

Participation is a form of recognition that is appreciated by persons at all levels of an organization. As other forms of recognition dry up because of potential conflicts of interest and ethics-code bans on receipt of gifts or entertainment beyond token value, managers have to be more attentive to legitimate forms of recognition. This can be a challenge. Anita Borek, a supervisor in a major medical center, told me that when regulators put tighter restrictions on health care vendors relative to gift giving, this meant a halt "to the small, token thank you gifts to the little guy working on the front line in the hospital. I have never known anyone who received an extravagant gift or entertainment, yet now, as a hospital supervisor, I'm scrambling to fill the appreciation void that the vendors previously filled." She added that this situation reminded her of grade school "when the whole class suffered for the disobedience of a few."

PRACTICAL WORKPLACE PARTICIPATION

From several conversations with Chris Lowney, who spent seventeen years as an investment banker with J.P. Morgan, I have gained an appreciation of the way participation can foster courage and thus affect, for the good, the quality of ethical decision making in an organization.

In recalling an ethical dilemma he faced at J.P. Morgan, Lowney told me about a proposed financial transaction that had financial merits as well as "the ancillary benefit of saving our company quite a considerable amount of money by reducing our tax liabilities. We asked for and received solid tax and accounting opinions from highly reputable outside firms that endorsed the proposed transaction." Then he recounted how, according to custom, "A number of us met, reviewed the opinions, asked ourselves if we would feel okay if the transaction showed up in the *New York Times*, and tentatively decided to go forward." Lowney kept turning that decision over in his mind. "A day later I visited my boss, who had also attended the meeting. I said something like, 'You know, on second thought, I just don't feel right about this.' My boss said nothing for a few seconds. Then he said, 'You know, neither do I. Let's take a pass on this one.' "

This was not the decision of an ethics officer; it was the result of open participation by colleagues, superiors, and subordinates, who trusted one another. In unpacking the decision, Lowney pointed out that there was a process at work that included some "best practices" employed by his firm. "We solicited external professional input as needed, in our case from tax and legal professionals. But we didn't allow those external opinions to absolve us of the responsibility for making and owning the decision ourselves. Soliciting an external advisor's opinion was *input* for a decision, not equivalent to *making* an ethical decision," he said with the indicated emphasis. And he added:

> Part of our corporate culture was the impulse to widen the circle of participants when faced with an important decision of any kind, including in the discussion those who might bring varying perspectives and professional points of view. And finally, we didn't decide by the seat

of our pants but had a specific forum in which to debate the decision in some kind of systematic way.

The decision, however, was overturned, but this too was part of the process, although, Lowney admits, it would probably not be considered "best practice" by academic analysts. It allowed for second thoughts and for representation. Here is how Lowney explains it:

> First, I re-opened in a side meeting with my boss a matter that apparently had already been decided, a practice that can lead to confusion and resentment among the group of decision makers. Second, when I spoke with my boss, neither of us articulated specific reasons for our viewpoints. I'm not holding myself up to be an ethical hero because it's possible that the decision he and I reached, not to go forward, was actually the wrong decision. Had he and I sorted through our reasoning behind our gut feelings, it's possible we might have become entirely comfortable with the proposed transaction.

So Lowney went on to explore what he believed was happening underneath the process.

> My boss and I kept thinking about the transaction after the meeting because in some way or another I took the decision personally: I cared enough not to feel good about what we were doing, and my personal ethical barometer was not satisfied merely by having gone through the group-meeting step of the process. What's more, I couldn't have had the conversation with my boss if I didn't trust him. And finally, he wouldn't have given my misgivings much currency if I hadn't established a track record for judgment and integrity that counted for something with him.

For Lowney, the "catch-22" of ethical dilemmas is that trust and integrity are tested during moments of crisis, "but trust and integrity are generally not established and won at the moment of crisis but in the months and years of ordinary decisions and work that *precede* the crisis. I worked at J.P. Morgan for seventeen years, and such moments of crisis probably occupied no more than one- or two-percent of my working life. Still, my values were equally relevant to my work the other ninety-nine percent of the time."

Not to be missed is the point that participation "in the months and years of ordinary decisions" served to build the trust and courage that produced an ethical decision in a moment of crisis.

ETHICS IN A PARTICIPATORY WORKPLACE

All 160,000 employees of the Boeing Company receive a copy of the *Boeing Ethical Business Conduct Guidelines* booklet that opens with a full-page list of "Our Values." Included on this list are two items that relate to the principle of participation. The first is "people working together," and it is explained in these words: "We recognize our strength and our competitive advantage is and always will be—people. We will continually learn, and share ideas and knowledge. We will encourage cooperative efforts at every level and across all activities in our company."

Another Boeing value is "a diverse and involved team." This means "We value the skills, strengths, and perspectives of our diverse team. We will foster a participatory workplace that enables people to be involved in making decisions about their work."

I talked about ethics with Bonnie Soodick, senior vice president in Boeing's Office of Internal Governance. She is, in effect, the company's chief ethics officer. She is understandably embarrassed, but not overly defensive, in the face of ethical lapses of "the one or two percent of Boeing people who fall short of our standards." All employees are required, she said, to sign each year and abide by the "Boeing Code of Conduct." Those who work in finance have an additional "Code of Conduct for Finance" that must be understood, signed, and adhered to. Commitment to the principle of participation, as Boeing articulates it, is, she thinks, a positive influence toward their maintenance of expected ethical behavior. I did not think to ask her then, because it only occurred to me later, but I wonder if Boeing's notorious ethical lapses at the top (two successive CEOs, Harry C. Stonecipher, ousted by the board in 2005 for an inappropriate "personal relationship" with a female Boeing executive, and his predecessor, Philip M. Condit, who was forced to resign in 2003 for ethical lapses including extramarital affairs and inattention to contracting irregularities) might have been prevented had there been closer business interaction on their part—participation—with other Boeing decision makers.

In both my December 2004 interview with him and in his book about his five years as IRS Commissioner,[10] former American Management Systems (AMS) CEO Charles Rossotti stressed the importance of participation. His was a walk-around style of management that he brought with him from AMS to IRS and he regarded it as "a creative way to activate participation."

The walk-around style—getting close to the customer as well as to others at all levels of your organization—is, for him, a "management principle," which he distinguishes from "inviolable" ethical principles. Management principles "are flexible, what's needed, what works." People on the "front lines" at IRS, he found, "had come to believe that the people at the top were not connected to them and to the reality of the pressures that they were facing every day."

Rossotti told me:

What was ironic at IRS was that all the upper level managers, with very few exceptions, had worked their way up from the bottom. Very few were parachuted in from outside. But the thing is, when they hit a certain level, they got caught up in budgeting and administration and really had no involvement with others. There are some peculiar things about the tax business that reinforced this. So one of the things I was trying to achieve by going out to field offices and to meetings with taxpayers was not only to get a better feel myself for what was going on, but to try to get others in the IRS to start doing it too.

Among the "ground rules" that he set for the decision-making process within the organization was *"Sharing information widely*: Information produced by the teams [which he initiated] would be shared with people inside and outside the IRS, and comments would be solicited from the widest possible audience before decisions were made."[11]

Rossotti viewed internal communications as "a vital part of the change process," and there was a lot that he wanted to change when he became commissioner in 1997. Here are words from his first message to IRS employees:

An important part of teamwork is honest and open communication with each other and with Congress and the public. We cannot solve problems that we do not acknowledge.

As an initial step, I plan to spend as much time as possible over the next two months meeting with you and especially learning about the front-line work in the districts and service centers. I invite you to send me your views on matters that you think will be helpful to me in learning about the IRS and how it can work better.[12]

His commitment to "honest and open communication" paved the way for change at IRS that affected all "stakeholders"— taxpayers, Congress, the Treasury Department, and IRS employees at all levels of the organization. "[W]e developed a slogan to summarize the approach that worked best in dealing with stakeholders: 'Engage, then decide.' We tried first to share information and options with affected stakeholders before making a decision; then we tried to make a clear decision. The contrasting approach, 'Decide, then explain,' meaning to decide secretly and then to try to explain the decision to the people affected, usually didn't work."

Rossotti says he has "never been a believer in recipes and formulas for success in management" because the "facts of each situation are too diverse and the application of principles is often not easy to discern." Moreover, sometimes "valid principles conflict with each other and there is no really good solution, just a practical choice." He ends his book, however, with a solid set of nine management principles that he brought with him from AMS to IRS; they are "basic beliefs about what works in leading an organization during a period of change."[13] All nine are worth quoting, but here are just a few: "Successful change requires the right measurements and incentives." "Successful change requires knowing what is really going on where it counts—at the front line." "Successful change requires open and honest communication inside and outside the organization."

I would simply add that successful change requires effective and widespread participation.

Few think about widening participation to the extent advocated by John Emrick, CEO of Oregon-based Norm Thompson Outfitters, who insists that "we welcome the customer into the room" whenever key decisions are being made. The imaginary presence and participation of the customer in a firm's otherwise secret and strategic meetings has an extraordinary leveling effect (in an on-the-level sense) on business decisions.

Now that globalization is a common characteristic of life in the new corporate culture, more and more decision makers are aware of themselves as part of a global enterprise that is running seven days a week, twenty-four hours a day. Decisions made by others whom they will never meet in person affect the decisions they are about to make. Because decision makers in a given organization are spread all around the world, operating in so many different cultures and languages, it is important that they have some common ground. They now have to get to "know one another," not through direct personal contact, but through shared criteria for making decisions. Participation is made possible for them not only through global communication, but, more importantly, through knowledge of and commitment to the principles that drive the organization's decisions, wherever that organization happens to be operating.

DECISION MAKING BY "DIAGONAL SLICE"

Ryuzaburo Kaku, former chairman of Canon, the Japanese technology company, has observed that global companies have no future if the earth has no future, so it is in their interest to work together to attempt to solve global problems. How can global companies promote peace and prosperity, he asks, and still meet their profit-producing responsibilities? The answer, he says, "is *kyosei*, which can best be defined as a 'spirit of cooperation,' in which individuals and organizations live and work together for the common good."[14] The cooperative spirit that would take a company beyond its own national boundaries to cooperate with other transnational companies should begin, however, within the company itself. And this involves recognition and application of the principle of participation. Kaku writes of the Canon experience: "A company that practices *kyosei* must start by creating a cooperative spirit among its employees. At Canon, we manage the company on the principle that there are no distinctions between factory and office workers. Everyone is a *sha-in*, which translates as 'member of the company.' "

Canon started cooperating with workers early in its history, well before other Japanese companies. In 1943, Canon eliminated the distinction between salaried and hourly workers and did away with the rule that they had to use different cafeterias and restrooms.[15]

Even in more formal and highly structured companies like

IBM and Xerox, participation is essential. "Very little can be accomplished in the workplace without it," said former Xerox vice chairman Bill Glavin, when I asked for his views. Although the example he gave related to participation at the top—between him and David Kearns, the chairman—Glavin's experience at both IBM and Xerox sold him on the importance of participation. Glavin and Kearns worked together and were friends at IBM before moving—Glavin went first and encouraged Kearns to follow—to Xerox.

When Glavin became vice chairman, he asked his old friend and now boss Kearns, "What do you want me to bring to you for pre-approval?" Kearns said he wanted to review any project involving more than $15 million, and any change in status for persons reporting directly to Glavin. "Just talk to me first."

Some time later, in the face of declining market share, Glavin had an important strategy meeting with his top eight reports. They discussed the introduction of a new product that would not be ready for market for another year or so. "What would happen," Glavin wondered aloud, "if we dropped existing product prices now in order to hold market share until we introduced the new '10 Series' products?" Glavin and his top associates decided that prices on existing products should be dropped by 40 to 60 percent. This would mean at least a half-billion loss in profit. Moreover, the plan would be to bring the new product to market, when ready, at these lower prices.

It happened to be a Tuesday when Glavin took the plan to Kearns for further discussion. "How sure are you of the numbers?" Kearns asked. "We feel good about them," said Glavin. "Okay, I'll need a couple of days to review it."

On the following Friday, they met again and Kearns said, "Let's do it; it's the right thing to do." He told Wall Street what they had decided. This happened in 1982. The company was able to hold market share and indeed rebuild it so that by 1989, Xerox was back where it wanted to be. "It was a half-billion dollar loss, but it saved the company," said Glavin, "and the point of recounting it now is to repeat that it was the right thing to do. Many people, even when they know what is right, just don't do it."

Merlin Olson, who began his career as a hospital administrator, later joined the Deloitte & Touche consulting group where he became a partner with wide consulting experience in many industries. He talked to me about decision making by "diagonal slice." He illustrated the meaning of that phrase by sketching the typical organizational chart. The industry, firm, and job titles do not matter for purposes of this illustration, he said. You have the Board on top of the chart; the CEO immediately below; then a line of several VPs; under them another line filled with department-head boxes; under that a line of supervisors; and at bottom a wider line of boxes for staff positions. The "diagonal slice," representing participatory decision making, runs down one side on the chart. It is diagonal because there are fewer boxes on the higher tiers of the organization. So the "slice" picks up a vice president, a department head, a supervisor, and at least one staff member. They constitute a decision-making group. "For an important corporate policy decision," says Olson, "a CEO will get the best input and advice by appointing a committee or task force with members representing the 'diagonal slice.' This produces multiple views and perspectives—all valid. Each level can make important contributions. Each person must be made to feel comfortable and valued as a participant."

Even when the subject matter must remain confidential, Olson believes it is important to seek input from all levels. This fosters a corporate culture that encourages two-way, up-and-down communication.

Not everything that happens around the table—one of the images I will offer below for a summary of this principle—is ethical. That point was made in separate cartoons that friends, knowing I was at work on this book, have sent me. One shows a conspicuously empty chair at a conference table and has the person seated at the head saying, "It's just us today; Campbell called in ethical." The other depicts a boss saying to those seated around him: "Of course what we're doing is wrong, but that doesn't make it indefensible." The executive who sent me this cartoon added, in his own hand, "Not uncommon—especially for lawyers."

For a takeaway image of the principle of participation, think of a large round table. Go back to King Arthur, if you wish, or think of the tables you see in large boardrooms or smaller conference rooms. A modification of this image, more congenial perhaps to those whose working days are not spent in skyscrapers, is a large workbench with a rougher surface, sturdier legs, and wooden benches for seating space, not leather chairs. Whether round table or workbench, the image suggests sufficient space to accommodate all those responsible for the quality of whatever it is that emerges from the production process. The point, of course, is that everyone deserves a place at the table or the workbench. All have a right not to be shut out from the decision making that affects the conditions and the outcomes of their work. Some might want to project this imagery out into a computer or telecommunications network. That's fine so long as the possibility of a good connection is available to all.

CHAPTER EIGHT

Commitment

Here again the issue of trust is in the foreground. Inevitably, when journalistic accounts of the new corporate culture touch upon the human side of downsizing, you will read that corporate loyalty is a thing of the past. Corporations no longer keep their commitments, the story usually goes. And often that is exactly the case. John Nahas, president of U.S. Bank Nebraska, told me in 2003 that "the most dramatic change I've seen in business is the disappearance of loyalty on both sides—the organization and the employee."

Lou Giraudo makes a distinction between big and small business in discussing the disappearance of commitment from the world of contemporary business.

We've put such a premium on financial success that loyalty, fidelity, and reliability are not real values in the minds of many anymore. Big business neither gives nor rewards those values today, so big business has become a revolving door. Share price, options, and exit have replaced commitment and loyalty. Young executives and professionals flip from company to company because I, me, and my pocket take precedence over everything else. The problem may be more urgent for small business, however, because small business cannot survive without commitment flowing in both directions, from employees to company and company to employees.

"Commitment stays the course," says Cynthia Danaher. Merlin Olson ties commitment to superior performance. "Everyone should meet expectations," he says, "the most valuable team members are those who consistently exceed expectations—that's commitment."

"Trust no one, except your family," an unemployed vice president of an automotive services company told me when I interviewed him after he lost his job in the wake of a downsizing decision. Many men and women in similar situations will tell you that they will never again put the interests of an organization before their own, they will not trust employers to keep their word, and they will not trust co-workers not to "do them in" if the downsizing wheels start to turn, and the employment rolls are certain to be reduced.

Commitments are the cement of social relationships. If commitments are kept in the workplace, morale and a sense of security will be high. If a firm simply cannot make commitments to its employees, uncertainty, anxiety, and the individual's commitment to self-preservation will increase in the best of hearts and the best of workplaces. Because fewer and fewer firms are able in this new corporate culture to promise permanent employment, closer and completely honest communication is all the more necessary if trust is to be preserved in the workplace. Once trust erodes, productivity suffers, and the enterprise is in danger of collapsing into the debris of broken commitments. Hence, the importance in any business organization of the ethical principle of keeping commitments. Management consultant Tom Saporito thinks that commitment is "one of the more challenging principles to translate into one's work." It is critically important to do so, however, "because meaning in life is derived from the concept of commitment—from being able to commit to someone or something like family, spouse, a set of beliefs." Without commitment," he says, "you're going to come up empty in the search for meaning in that large slice of your life that is identified with the workplace."

GOOD COMPANIONSHIP MAKES FOR
GOOD COMPANIES

Related to the ability to keep commitments are the personal characteristics of dependability and reliability. If these disappear from the workplace, there will be a morale problem on the production side, and it is virtually certain that product and service quality will also diminish. This, of course, means there will be a demand-side problem of customer discontent leading to negative economic consequences. A good company should mean good companionship—human beings working together in a social organization which, like a healthy human body, works well when all the members are contributing profitably (and enjoying the process as well). Here, as in the application of all the other principles under review, there is a reminder that good ethics means good business. This is an appropriate point to move this reflection on to the notion of trust.

The journal of the Public Relations Society of America is *The Public Relations Strategist*. The cover of the Fall 2003 issue calls attention to "Corporate America's New Secret Weapon: Trust." The cover story, written by Joanne DeLavan Reichardt, vice president of corporate communications and public affairs for Ranstad North America, opens as follows: "Trust has seldom been more top of mind in America's break rooms, board rooms and corner offices than it is now. In fact, we are in the midst of a crisis of confidence when it comes to trust, one that has profound implications for us as social human beings and as professional communicators." The article goes on to say that mistrust is pervasive. "We've seen it in politics, with special favors exchanged for political contributions. We've seen it in sports, with investigations of cheating or lying by university coaches and Little League teams that falsify birth certificates of star players. We've certainly seen it in business, with accounting fraud scandals."[1]

Both culture and trust are on the minds of business observers today. Questions like these are being raised by friendly critics: What is the dominant value that defines a given business culture? How widely is that value shared throughout the organization? How trustworthy are the leaders in an organization? How trustworthy are they perceived to be by those they lead in that organization? How fully encompassing is the trust that generates the energy and purifies the air of the organization that has a claim on the time, talent, and commitment of anyone on the payroll?

BEING FAITHFUL TO KNOWN VALUES

John Gardner thought that our society is not suffering from confusion about values, but from infidelity to the values we know we should hold and share if ours is going to be a good society.[2] The ideals of freedom, equality of opportunity, human dignity, justice, and related values are well known to us and widely shared. We are not, however, sufficiently committed to them to let them shape our social behavior. "The fact that we are not always faithful to these shared values," writes Gardner, "does not indicate confusion nor a failure of the consensus. *We know the values to which we are being unfaithful.*"[3]

Lynn Paine translates this same idea into the practical business setting.

> Even such generally accepted ethical principles as keeping promises need to be validated as organizational principles, not just as personal commitments. Individuals must know these principles are relevant at work and that others know it, too. Otherwise, some may mistakenly think they are alone in their beliefs and set these values aside in misguided deference to others. Of course, simply stating a principle is not sufficient to validate it. Validation occurs through practice and over time as the prin-

ciple is seen to be an integral and operative force in the organization's activities.[4]

In other words, commitment is both an organizational and a personal ethical principle. The organization, in all its inter-communicating parts, must know and honor commitment—to delivery dates, to quality standards, and to similar "prom-ises" on which divisions within the organization, as well as outside clients or customers, can depend. The application of this principle of commitment in a business setting will make "promise keepers" of all who work there. That can be noth-ing but good for business.

The Boeing Company's "Code of Conduct" does not men-tion commitment, but in explanatory question-and-answer notes attached to the code and distributed to all employees, Boeing stresses commitment as a safeguard to unethical use of knowledge gained by previous employment with a com-pany that now competes with Boeing. Question: "I used to work for XYZ Company, a current competitor of Boeing. Can I brief my team on XYZ's proposal strategies?" Answer: "No. You have a commitment to protect confidential information of your former employer, and that commitment does not cease when you leave that company. Boeing does not want infor-mation that it does not have a right to have. You need to disclose your prior relationship to your immediate manager and to abide by all obligations of confidentiality owed to your former employer." Some commitments just never go away.

Charles Rossotti was IRS Commissioner from 1997 to 2002. He has written about that experience in his book[5] I mentioned in the last chapter. It is sufficiently autobiographical to give the reader a good understanding of his introduction to busi-ness through his parents' family-owned business, and his ap-proach to management as co-founder and longtime CEO of AMS. When I interviewed him for this book, I learned how important he considers relationships to be in the success of an organization, and how much distrust he found at IRS when he became commissioner. He had observed his parents, who ran a small business together, and noticed how their success was built on trusting relationships forged with suppliers, employees, and customers. The strength of their personal relationships led to the success he and a few friends enjoyed when they launched the consulting firm AMS. But when he arrived at IRS, he found a situation that is neatly described by the title he gave to Chapter 6 of his book: "So Many People, So Much Distrust: Rebuilding Relationships."

"The IRS situation was completely at odds with what I had learned in my parents' businesses long ago and had applied in my twenty-eight years with AMS: that relationships of trust were the cornerstones of success. Here at IRS we had relationships of distrust. And they were the root cause of many failures."[6] Lack of trust magnified every problem, he said. "How," he asked, "were we going to turn the tide of distrust that impeded progress across the whole IRS?" His answer: "Building on the good relationships, and rebuilding the ones that are broken, is the key to regaining trust throughout the organization"[7]

Writes Rossotti:

> As a critical first step in reversing the IRS's "death spiral of distrust," I could personally work on building relationships with a circle of people who were most important to the functioning of the IRS. Over time, we could expand this circle by setting up the IRS so more and more of IRS management built more and more direct, trusting relationships with people inside and outside the agency. Over time, we could replace the abstraction of management with meaningful relationships of one person to another.[8]

Well, he could and he did. I will relate more of what he did to improve things at IRS in Chapter 11 of this book; for now, the point to note is the building or rebuilding of relationships strengthens commitment, and commitment is the infrastructure of trust.

KEEPING COMMITMENTS ON THE GROUND
AND OUT IN CYBERSPACE

I was struck by an advertisement placed in the *Washington Post* on June 16, 2003, by Consumer WebWatch, a project of Consumers Union, publisher of *Consumer Reports*. It listed 29 Web-based businesses over the following statement:

> The companies listed above have made a commitment to our five basic guidelines that help prevent confusion, deception, and fraud on the Internet. We will continue to publish the names of those Web sites that deserve praise for their commitment to the consumer, and to disclose those sites that show a lack of commitment. We're Consumer WebWatch, a part of Consumers Union, publisher of *Consumer Reports*. We're here to improve your online experience, so you can seek information and shop online with more trust and confidence. Check with us at www.ConsumerWebWatch.org. Or call 1-914-378-2600.

I was struck, of course, by the repeated use of the word "commitment" and amused by the open threat to get the offenders in line by doing what Woodrow Wilson said the federal government would do in 1914 when it set up the Federal Trade Commission, namely, "punish with pitiless publicity." The five basic guidelines mentioned in the advertisement were:

(1) Identity: "Web sites should clearly disclose the physical location where they are produced;"

(2) Advertising and Sponsorships: "Sites should clearly distinguish advertising from news and information;"

(3) Customer Service: "Sites engaged in consumer transactions should clearly disclose relevant financial relationships with other sites, particularly when these relationships affect the cost to a consumer;"

(4) Corrections: "Sites should diligently seek to correct false, misleading or incorrect information;" and

(5) Privacy: "Site privacy policies should be easy to find and clearly, simply stated."

Without commitment to these guidelines, the other ethical values that should be operative in Web-based businesses will not get the oxygen they need to survive.

Philip Merrill, whose experience ranges from magazine and newspaper publishing to service as president and chairman of the Export-Import Bank of the United States, thinks that "business is really about two things: (1) setting an objective and taking the steps necessary to reach it; and (2) extracting a promise and holding people to that promise." The "promise" almost always looks to the long run. "I've found that when you do things that are right for the long run, you are much more likely to come out better in the short run"—hence, the importance of getting and keeping people committed over the long haul.

Most people, he has found, "genuinely want to do the right thing. Where they trip up is when two worthy goals collide—worthy goals, not good or bad—worthy goals like paying people well and keeping costs down." You are committed to both, so you have to decide. Commitment, as Merrill sees it, is closely tied to character, which is the locus of sound decision making. Both character and commitment are needed to keep an operation successful and ethical over the long run. The relatively few business managers who, in Merrill's experience, are not committed to doing the right thing are typically not persons of character. They will not be helped, he thinks, by a book or course of instruction on ethics.

So he wonders if and how either commitment or character can be taught in an ethics class. Reflecting on Enron, he said: "Booking future revenues now in order to justify a bonus, or borrowing $600 million from your own company to buy stock as though your company were a piggy bank, or using corporate assets for excessively personal luxuries, are not actions that could have been controlled by reading a book on ethics." He did, however, say to me, "If your book can shed some light on all this, I would love to read it. Meanwhile, I'll continue to try to learn what's right by surrounding myself with people of character."

I had hoped that both he and his circle of friends would enjoy this book and recommend it to others. They would, in effect, be recommending themselves. Sadly, however, Phil Merrill lost his life in a boating accident on the Chesapeake Bay on June 10, 2006.

Hubert F. Gordon is a computer services contractor who thinks commitment is closely related to integrity—somewhat the same connection Merrill made between commitment and character. Gordon's work experience, first in the executive branch of state government, later as a private contractor doing business with the state, prompts him to think of commitment in terms of roles and obligations. In the workplace, he says, commitment "is related to the explicit and implicit set of obligations that exist between employer and employee, and between customer and vendor. These expectations have to be formalized and understood before you can begin to hope that commitments will be kept."

Former managing partner of McKinsey & Co., Fred Gluck, believes in the importance of commitment, but, as he reminded me, "One needs to be careful of what commitments to make, and one must recognize that such principles as integrity, veracity, and human dignity take precedence over commitment." This is a good point and a helpful reminder that not all principles are equal.

Speaking generally from his extensive experience as head of McKinsey, Gluck told me:

I don't believe the challenges to principled behavior occur primarily in the business context. My experience is that the vast majority of people involved in business are well-intentioned and demonstrate integrity in most situations. There are deviations from principled behavior in all aspects of life—take politics and organized religion for example. Perhaps the most egregious examples of unprincipled behavior in recent years occurred in our own church with the reality and mishandling of the sex-abuse scandals.

Another very good point.

Joe Kraemer, who runs the Washington office of Law and Economics Consulting Group, told me, "I give and expect 110 percent whenever it is needed. This can mean staff meetings at six in the morning and travel on little notice. Those who cannot or will not make that kind of a commitment will not survive here over the long run. On the other hand, given that stress times come and go, when we have down periods, I urge the team to take three-day weekends, and I'm very liberal with time off." This approach serves to remind that we are talking about human beings, not robots, when we are talking about commitment and other expressions of principled behavior in business. You can repair a robot when it breaks down and take subsequent care not to run it, as we say, into the ground. But humans are different. They, too, can break down if overworked, so care must be taken not to make excessive demands. When humans act inconsistently with their positive ethical principles (a moral breakdown, if you will), you can only forgive while expecting recommitment to doing the right thing. If that recommitment is not forthcoming, or if no genuine commitment was there in the first place, there is no longer room in the ethical organization for the uncommitted person.

In the several conversations I had with Joe Kraemer, he made occasional mention of the influence his army experience had on his managerial style. He learned, however, that "command and control" was not the way to go in business, but introducing order and strategic planning to the organization was most appropriate. Ken Sparks, of the Federal City Council, was a Marine fighter pilot. Not surprisingly, he acknowledges that the "esprit" of the Marine Corps is still with him. When he hears commitment, he thinks, *Semper Fidelis*.

I asked Robert Reed, CEO of Omaha-based Physicians Mutual Insurance Company, if he was noticing different shades of commitment in the younger people now coming into his organization. His reply: "I am so pleased with what I see in the young people coming up in our organization. I think they are committed. Commitment means seeing something beyond yourself—a noble purpose, a belief in the purpose of your organization. It also means humble service. We are so lucky; I feel so good about the young people we have coming up." That indeed is encouraging to hear!

Reed told me something else that might help to attract committed young people to Physicians Mutual. "We make it mandatory for all our managers to do community service. We get some resistance, and we're prepared to make exceptions or give them a pass for a year. But we think community service is very important. We're not an island at 24th and Dodge, watching the whole thing go by."

Someone once remarked to me that the world is made up of three kinds of people—those who make things happen, those who know what's happening, and those who don't have a clue as to what is going on. The clueless are the uncommitted.

I referred earlier to the philosophical bent of Jack Conroy. His practical side comes through, however, in discussing commitment. "Commitment to what?" he asks. If it is only to one's personal benefit and goals, "then a critical element of corporate governance is missing; significant problems are on their way." Within the organization there has to be commitment, he believes, to the organization's basic values, "assuming them to be fair, just, and appropriate." He thinks corporate officers have to show their commitment "to the entire organization by working for the common good of the entity, and employees are expected to express a reciprocal commitment. This is a corollary to the principle of integrity." In combination, commitment and integrity will, he believes, keep labor unrest low and compensation levels reasonable.

In discussing integrity in Chapter 3, I offered excerpts from a speech given at the National Press Club in the wake of the corporate scandals by the Dean of the Harvard Business School (HBS). He was questioned then, as I indicated, by an alumnus of HBS who appeared to be skeptical about the school's ability to form students into persons of integrity. That question prompted Dean Kim Clark to link integrity with commitment and to point out how commitment in the teacher is a precondition to the cultivation of commitment in the student:

> The first thing you have to do as a teacher is to decide how you feel; and you have to, as a teacher, decide in your own heart what your own commitments are personally. And that commitment comes with you into the classroom. And that's the foundation—to make sure that we in the school, those of us who have the responsibility to teach—that we really believe and are committed to the kind of objectives that I talked about, so that we are committed to educating leaders with those kind of characteristics. So it starts inside the teacher, it starts inside the dean, if you will.

Similarly, doing the right thing in business—acting ethically—starts inside the decision maker. Internalized principles are all it takes to get the ethical engine moving.

A useful image to associate with the principle of commitment is the old familiar padlock. Either open, or already snapped in place, the inverted-u-shaped metal ring at the top says to the world that something is, or is about to be, locked in place. Under lock and key. Done deal. Put away for good. Committed.

CHAPTER NINE

Social Responsibility

Simply because it would be unfair to name the school, I will not identify the institution or the business leader who was both offended and scandalized to hear a faculty member from one of America's "best" business schools declare in a seminar for executives held on that campus: "We have no business teaching what's right and wrong; we don't know what's right and wrong. All we know is what's legal and illegal." That professor needs an introduction to the four-part model offered below that helps to explain the principle of social responsibility.

A FOUR-LEVEL SOCIAL RESPONSIBILITY MODEL

This four-level principle, as I indicated earlier, relates to the economic, legal, ethical, and discretionary or philanthropic categories of a firm's behavior. All four are important; in combination they explain what is often referred to as corporate social responsibility or good corporate citizenship. The agnostic professor, quoted above, never rose above level two.

At level one, economic responsibility will dictate some or all of the following steps at strategic moments and in strategic sequence: raising prices; lowering costs; deciding on workforce reduction in the interest of efficiency; ordering renewal or replacement of plant and equipment; introducing new technology; developing new products or services; discovery of new markets; and the assumption of risk. The economic objective of "lean" must, if the organization is to be responsible as well as responsive to economic signals, never become "mean," despite the rhetoric of the marketplace. Profitability must, this economic level of responsibility would insist, be maintained. This is not to say that profitability is to be maximized for shareholder return. There are stakeholders, other than shareholders, who have an interest in the economic health of the enterprise.

The point to emphasize at this first level—the foundational level—of social responsibility (and it is a point that is well received in even the most conservative quarters of the business community) is that no business can be socially responsible unless it is economically viable. What food is to an individual, profit is to a corporation—absolutely necessary in order to exist. It does not follow, however, that a firm should maximize its intake of profit any more than an individual should be encouraged to maximize his or her consumption of food. The goal of the corporation should be to maximize its long-term viability. Attention to the demands of good corporate citizenship, which, of course, means being socially responsible, serves to guarantee long-term viability.

The second level, legal responsibility in corporate life, means abiding by all laws and recognizing that regulatory law is there to maintain competition, that is, to assure fair prices and all the other competitive effects that would be produced by a perfectly free and smoothly functioning market made up of many sellers and buyers enjoying full information and freedom of resource movement. This is the *theory* of perfect competition. Where the reality is less than perfect, the law is there to maintain competitive outcomes. But there is more to it than that. To remain within the law is not the sum and substance of corporate responsibility; not everything that is required by ethics is also required by law. Conversely, even though an executive did not have criminal intent in cases of fraud and questionable accounting (as the defense lawyers will always argue when CEOs like Bernie Ebbers and Ken Lay are on trial), that is not to say they did nothing unethical. Fraud and "aggressive" accounting that result in billion-dollar losses to shareholders are always unethical, despite the fact that a clever defense lawyer may create "reasonable doubt" in the minds of jurors as to whether a defendant had "criminal intent," and thus the defendant might, on grounds of reasonable doubt, be found not guilty.

Ethical responsibility, the third level, stretches all the way from respect for individual human dignity (in employees, customers, suppliers, colleagues, competitors) on out to respect for the physical environment that is necessary to sustain life on this planet. The ethics issue is a character issue. Character is the answer to the question: What does it take to do the right thing in business or personal life? At this third level of corporate social responsibility—the ethical—troubling issues abound.

Countless ethical considerations come to mind, not all of them make the headlines. For example, there are serious ethical considerations that arise in the context of downsizing and the new corporate culture of economic uncertainty and contingent employment. One that I see as crucial belongs in the category of "employability" and it applies to both employer and employee. Keeping an employee employable is an ethical responsibility of both the employer and the employee in this new corporate culture. This means that the firm should assist, by paying for or providing training, all willing employees to enlarge their ensemble of skills and stay on the growing edge of employability in a marketable skill category. The employee has an ethical obligation to continue his or her education and training by contributing personal time and personal financial resources to the process. This can be viewed as a stewardship responsibility relating to the constructive use of both time and talent. It can also be viewed as the practice of prudence, preparing the way for the kind of fortune that favors the well-prepared.

Government, mindful of the principle of subsidiarity (to be discussed in Chapter 11), would do well to use its taxing powers to encourage both employer and employee to invest resources directed at maintaining and expanding employability. The primary ethical responsibility, however, is divided between the organization and those now on the payroll. Both will benefit from this kind of investment. The employee whose skills stay sharp will have less difficulty finding another job. The organization will enjoy increased productivity as long as the updated skills are available to it, that is, the updated skill holder is still on the payroll. When that dreaded day comes when the organization must trim its workforce, it does so knowing that it had done what it reasonably and responsibly could to give its people a leg up on the job search by enhancing their employability before they were released.

A whole array of other ethical issues, not to be explored here, faces anyone at work in the new corporate culture. New privacy issues have emerged as a function of the new workplace technology, where passwords and personal identification numbers cannot always be counted on to protect the privacy of voice mail and computer files. Employee Assistance Programs for victims of drug or alcohol abuse raise questions of confidentiality and career progress for those who voluntarily avail themselves of assistance programs. Readers interested in these and other new questions can track them down as they appear on almost any day in the business press.

The fourth level in this social responsibility model is the discretionary area of corporate social responsibility. Issues here rise above, so to speak, the economic, legal, and ethical; these are the "good" initiatives that should be taken but are not strictly required to keep the firm viable, or to stay within the law and the demands of ethical conduct. Reason-based ethics may make no demands at this higher level, but religious obligation well may require action. Philanthropic support for educational institutions, hospitals, churches, community organizations, the United Way, and other charities fit in here. "Love your neighbor" (often mentioned by respondents to my inquiries about corporate social responsibility) has to mean a lot more than just not doing harm to your neighbor. Religious conviction will often require you to walk the extra mile.

In discussing the new corporate culture, one major issue that fits here and, in the view of many, should bridge back into the strictly ethical area is the question of executive compensation. This is related, of course, to systemic behavior within capitalism: Thousands of employees are laid off, and the stock market reacts by boosting the stock price and, with it, stock-related income for top management. Should there be a "maximum wage" that puts a lid on the growing gap between average earnings of production workers and the pay of top management? Should top managers, particularly those who benefit from compensation windfalls in the wake of their own decisions to lay others off, be expected at this discretionary level to share their gain with those hurt by their downsizing decision? Perhaps the area that needs attention here is the bonus portion of the compensation package. Base salary may be in line, but bonuses have a way of bouncing out of control.

What, finally, at this discretionary, philanthropic, or voluntary community-responsibility level, can be expected of the economic "haves" with respect to job creation for those less fortunate—not necessarily for those who have given up or are unwilling to work, but for those who lose their jobs to progress in this new corporate culture? Clearly, there is an ethical responsibility to do something, and there may be an obligation in charity to do even more. In a knowledge economy (not simply an "information economy") like ours in this new corporate culture, the ethical imperative points not only to the care of casualties, but also to the advancement of education for the cultivation of new ideas, new creativity, new technology, new products, new services, and eventually, new jobs.

TYLENOL: A LESSON IN SOCIAL RESPONSIBILITY

In Chapter 3 of this book, I reported the views of former Johnson & Johnson CEO James Burke relative to integrity. It is interesting to note that David Collins, who was a member of the J&J executive strategy committee charged with handling the Tylenol crisis, chose to call that experience a "lesson in social responsibility." His September 27, 2002, lecture on this topic at the Vermont Law School was reprinted in the *Vermont Law Review* under the title, "A Lesson in Social Responsibility: Corporate Response to the 1980's Tylenol Tragedies."[1]

Collins states that the Tylenol capsules "were not defective when they were manufactured and sold. Nor was J&J under any legal obligation to do what it did. What it did, in other words, went beyond the legal mandates to respond to more demanding imperatives."[2] This serves to highlight the distinction between the "legal" and the "ethical" in the ascending four-level social responsibility model. J&J had no legal obligation, but it recognized a serious ethical obligation.

The "imperatives" Collins referred to are rooted in what General Robert Wood Johnson, longtime CEO of J&J, referred to in the early 1940s as "a new industrial philosophy." He articulated it in these words: "[I]t is in the enlightened self-interest of modern industry to realize that its service to its customers comes first, its service to its employees and management second, and its service to its stockholders last. It is to the enlightened self-interest of industry to accept and fulfill its full share of social responsibility."[3] Notice that "social responsibility" was in the vocabulary of a major industrialist back in the 1940s.

The general later spelled out the famous Johnson & Johnson Credo, to which Jim Burke referred as his indispensable guideline, and which deserves a place here in this discussion of corporate social responsibility. Note the nice summary of the concept of social responsibility in the third paragraph of this, the latest expression of the credo:[4]

Our Credo

We believe our first responsibility is to the doctors,
nurses and patients,
to mothers and fathers and all others who use our
products and services.

In meeting their needs, everything we do must be
of high quality.
We must constantly strive to reduce our costs
in order to maintain reasonable prices.
Customers' orders must be serviced promptly and
accurately.
Our suppliers and distributors must have an opportunity
to make a fair profit.

We are responsible to our employees,
the men and women who work with us throughout
the world.
Everyone must be considered as an individual.
We must respect their dignity and recognize their merit.
They must have a sense of security in their jobs.
Compensation must be fair and adequate,
and working conditions clean, orderly and safe.
We must be mindful of ways to help our employees
fulfill their family responsibilities.
Employees must feel free to make suggestions and
complaints.
There must be equal opportunity for employment,
development and advancement for those qualified.
We must provide competent management,
and their actions must be just and ethical.

We are responsible to the communities in which we live
and work and to the world community as well.
We must be good citizens—support good works and
charities and bear our fair share of taxes.
We must encourage civic improvements and better
health and education.
We must maintain in good order
the property we are privileged to use,
protecting the environment and natural resources.

Our final responsibility is to our stockholders.
Business must make a sound profit.

We must experiment with new ideas.
Research must be carried on, innovative programs
developed and mistakes paid for.
New equipment must be purchased, new facilities
provided and new products launched.
Reserves must be created to provide for adverse times.
When we operate according to these principles,
the stockholders should realize a fair return.

CONSERVATION, TRUST, AND RESPECT

Returning to the heart of the matter regarding social responsibility, and looking, if you will, into the heart of the person
trying to be socially responsible in business, I pick up two
points from my conversation with Ken Sparks, of the private
sector Federal City Council in Washington, DC. He told me
that he thinks the principle of human dignity "should be extended to nonhuman creatures and things, translating into
respect for nature and the conservation of natural resources."
Not surprisingly, then, when he reflected on the principle of
social responsibility, he said, "For me, this includes looking
at the full costs of one's behavior and taking societal costs
into account in decision making." And since much of his career was spent facilitating planning and execution of private-
public initiatives in the Washington, DC, metropolitan area,
his sensitivity to social responsibility directed his attention to
trends in urban development and the need to focus on "smart
growth" while curbing urban sprawl. He also thinks in terms
of the "triple bottom line," which includes "environmental
and financial" as adjectives that deserve a place alongside
"social" responsibility.

Paul Coughlin, who specializes in turnaround management,
says, "trust and respect are my two drivers." He thinks of
social responsibility as an integral part of justice. Social justice is a category that is congenial to his management outlook
because he finds himself, more often than not, dealing with
frightened workers who are the victims not just of circum-

stances, but sometimes of mismanagement. "Please help me save your jobs," he says in his opening talk at a troubled company. He talks about the "inherent value" of all present and publicly commits himself to the protection and promotion of that value. This, in Coughlin's view, is a work of justice. Because it extends to a workplace community of potentially unemployed people, he considers it to be not only socially responsible activity, but, in fact, a work of social justice.

Similarly, Tom Saporito, the organizational and search consultant, thinks of social responsibility as "akin" to the concept of fairness and justice. He thinks it requires "sensitivity to balancing the needs of internal and external constituencies that are not always well synchronized with one another."

From his long experience in the broadcast industry, where license renewal applications require a local station to assess the community's needs, Larry Herbster thinks in terms of "giving something back to the community" when he thinks of social responsibility. In other words, community needs help to set the agenda for the broadcasting business. It is not just the public's "need to know" that has to be met, but the community's "need to grow" and prosper. Broadcast properties provide electronic "public squares" and "village wells," where a sense of community can develop and information-exchanges necessary for sound public-policy formation can take place.

Chatting about these matters a few years ago with John (Hap) Fauth, founder and chairman of a diverse conglomerate of holdings known as the Churchill Companies, headquartered in Minneapolis, I picked up an expression that I have repeated often to business students in lectures on corporate social responsibility. "The community is my partner," said Hap Fauth. Acknowledging that his mission "is to create value for the people who work at Churchill, for our investors, and for the larger community," he made the point that granting "partnership" status to the community where you conduct your business will serve to keep you conscious of community needs and what you might be able to do, through your business, to meet them. That is a great way to think about the principle of social responsibility.

MISREPRESENTATION IS SOCIALLY IRRESPONSIBLE

In the first of a weeklong series of "After Enron" editorials that began on March 19, 2002, the *Washington Post* employed a useful analogy to explain how false financial disclosures in one firm can harm the larger society, hence, the social responsibility of that one firm (and its auditors) to make honest financial representations to the public. "Imagine a patient at a medical checkup," begins the *Post* editorial. "Let's say she's important. She runs a major company, or she runs in the Olympics. There's a lot riding on her health, so she gets wired up to a vast battery of medical equipment, and a team of high-priced doctors notes her pulse and blood pressure and other vital measurements. After long and learned study, the doctors pronounce the patient healthy and publish her charts to prove it. But the numbers in the charts turn out to be fictitious. The machines didn't work, and the doctors all knew it. The patient soon falls ill."

You can see where this is going. Public corporations—that is, those whose shares are publicly owned and traded on a stock exchange—have to get an annual checkup and publish the results. "These accounts—showing a firm's income, assets, and other vital statistics—allow the public to judge how much money the firm may make in the future and therefore what the firm is worth today. But the accounts often turn out to be dishonest. The health of the nation's economic system is at stake." The editorial then goes on to ask and answer a question of vital importance to the reading and investing public, indeed to society as a whole:

Why are financial disclosures so important? Because if they are misleading, the public will bid up the share price of dud companies, allowing them to raise cheap capital and waste it, and maybe take over sounder companies and wreck them as well. Meanwhile good firms will get commensurately less capital, so they'll grow more slowly. Fewer jobs will be created, and corporate profits will be lower—so there'll be less tax revenue to pay for public services and less new capital to finance fresh business investment. Savings will build up less quickly in workers' retirement accounts. On one estimate, Enron's implosion cost state pension systems about $3 billion.

That recitation echoes the old saying in college classrooms that in economics, nothing is certain, anything is possible, and everything depends on everything else. Interdependence is a fact of economic life. It is the transmission network through which the current of social responsibility or irresponsibility runs. An awareness of interdependence provides the soil for the growth of individual and corporate social consciousness.

In a conversation with Henry Hockeimer, a retired president of Ford Aerospace, who was also vice president of the motor company (he retired in 1985), I gained an interesting perspective on how social responsibility might take root in an individual conscience. He mentioned that from 1972 to 1975 he had responsibility for 5,000 employees at Ford's Connersville, Indiana, plant where parts for car air-conditioning units were manufactured. He recalled thinking to himself one day as he looked out over the employees' parking lot that, assuming an average family size of four, he was responsible for 20,000 lives. In addition to the 5,000 who worked for Ford, he thought to himself, there were spouses and children whose hopes and dreams, communities and schools, and so much more, were all tied into what he did every day on the job. He said he never forgot that day and the stretched vision of social responsibility that came to him in one reflective moment. The plant, now owned by Visteon Climate Control, is still a Ford supplier, although no longer owned by Ford.

Hockeimer also recalled, with some pride, another moment when a Ford executive gave him, some time after he had made a particularly tough decision, a small wooden plaque that had a Civil War-era pistol mounted on it above a metal plate inscribed with the words, "H.E. Hockeimer: A Straight Shooter."

At a Ford General Management Meeting in Newport Beach, California, in April 1985, Henry Hockeimer gave a speech that, he was amused years later to discover and mention to me, employed some of the same vocabulary that I have been using in this book: "We are dedicated to making our *commitments* to our customers, to our suppliers, to our stockholders, and to our employees. We are committed to *integrity* in dealing with our customers, our suppliers, our employees, and ourselves. We are committed to creating an environment which encourages *innovation, teamwork*, and *employee satisfaction*" (emphasis added in the notes the Hockeimer made available to me).

THE PARTNERSHIP BETWEEN PROFITABILITY AND SOCIAL RESPONSIBILITY

It has proved interesting to me, as I have talked to many business executives and read much management literature over the past several years, that business leaders are less articulate in describing their (and their organization's) broad societal responsibilities, than they are on insisting on "doing the right thing" personally and corporately in business. They are, however, widening their perspective gradually. Recall from Chapter 1 of this book the difficulties George Lodge encountered in communicating an understanding of "communitarian" values to mid-career business executives who were students in his Advanced Management Program classes at Harvard Business School thirty years ago. Business today is far more socially responsible than was the case back then, but business executives, by and large, do not yet have the vocabulary to explain its meaning and importance. Some, I think, are fearful of being labeled "liberal" or being seen as deserters from the ranks of rugged individualism.

This is why it was timely in 2003 for the *Harvard Business Review* paperback series to add to its list the following title:

"Harvard Business Review on Corporate Responsibility." A promotional paragraph on the back cover of this volume is intended to be reassuring to prospective business readers. It makes the point that profitability and social responsibility can indeed form a productive partnership.

> What and whom is a business for? This collection of articles gathers the latest thinking on the strategic significance of corporate social responsibility. Readers will develop an understanding of why businesses should continue to give money away even while laying off workers, how companies play a leadership role in solving today's social problems by incorporating the best thinking of government and nonprofit institutions, and how community needs are actually opportunities to develop ideas and demonstrate business technologies. Readers will see how corporate responsibility can lead to new markets and solutions to long-standing business problems.

If the Harvard Business School says it is okay to talk openly in corporate board rooms and executive suites about corporate social responsibility, it must be okay—or so it seems a growing number of men and women in business are beginning to think. They encountered a bit of a bump on the road to this dawning realization, however, in the pages of the January 22, 2005, issue of *The Economist*, a British publication with typically excellent coverage of the American business scene. The cover headline in that issue reads: "The Good Company: A Sceptical Look at Corporate Social Responsibility." Inside, the fourteen-page "special report" expresses the opinion that it is "a pity" that "the movement for corporate social responsibility has won the battle of ideas." It then goes on to argue unconvincingly that "companies that merely compete and prosper make society better off."

This view was anticipated by Steve Hilton and Giles Gibbons, founders of Britain's first social marketing company, whose book, *Good Business: Your World Needs You,* has a chapter on "Responsibility" that includes this concise summary of the critique:[5]

> Interestingly, it's possible to detect an emerging critique of corporate social responsibility, which also lasers in anxiously on what constitutes a desirable mix of state and business roles, but from the free market right rather than the radical left. A significant body of opinion is explicitly hostile to the idea that companies should do anything other than maximize profits while obeying the law. Those that support this line of thinking take their cue from the Nobel Prize-winning economist Milton Friedman who wrote: "Few trends could so thoroughly undermine the very foundations of our free society as the acceptance by corporate officials of a social responsibility other than to make as much money for their stockholders as possible. This is a fundamentally subversive doctrine. If businessmen do have a social responsibility other than making maximum profits for stockholders, how are they to know what it is? Can self-selected private individuals decide what the social interest is?"

The debate will doubtless continue. After their own discussion of the debate, Hilton and Gibbons conclude: "Enron shows us, in the most dramatic possible way, the importance of openness, transparency, and the need to embed the principles of social responsibility at every level of the corporate hierarchy."[6] I certainly agree and invite the undecided reader to continue to think about social responsibility as he or she moves into the next chapter, a consideration of the common good.

CRITIQUE FROM THE LEFT

Before moving there, however, take a moment to consider a critique of corporate social responsibility that comes from the left. As the subtitle to his book suggests, Joel Bakan's primary concern is with the corporation itself, not simply with corporate social responsibility. His book, *The Corporation: The Pathological Pursuit of Profit and Power,*[7] argues that "the corporation is a pathological institution, a dangerous possessor of the great power it wields over people and societies."[8] Corporate environmental and social responsibility are, says Bakan, "branding themes" that serve marketing purposes, help to give a given corporation some legitimacy, and mitigate the damage that corporations, by their very nature, inevitably do. Enron, he points out, produced a Corporate Responsibility Annual Report, "but was unable to continue its good works after it collapsed under the weight of its executives' greed, hubris, and criminality."[9] Here, in summary, is this author's grim view of the American corporation:

> As a psychopathic creature, the corporation can neither recognize nor act upon moral reasons to refrain from harming others. Nothing in its legal makeup limits what it can do to others in pursuit of its selfish ends, and it is compelled to cause harm when the benefits of doing so outweigh the costs. Only pragmatic concern for its own interests and the laws of the land constrain the corporation's predatory instincts, and often that is not enough to stop it from destroying lives, damaging communities, and endangering the planet as a whole.[10]

This negative, deterministic, pessimistic outlook is understandable perhaps, but, in my view, unwarranted in view of the character and the potential for good in business men and women and the institutions they, with state approval, create to serve their business purposes. An institution is simply a "way of doing things." Just as an individual without a bone structure would be an inert puddle of flesh on the floor, a group of individuals organized for a business purpose would, without a corporate structure, be like an unfocused, uncontrollable collection of oranges or marbles rolling across the floor. Once organized in a corporate structure, those individuals can work their will on both their internal organization and external environment by making decisions that are driven, not by expediency or any lesser motive, but by the principles, including the principle of social responsibility, that are outlined in this book.

For an image of social responsibility, consider the ripple effect caused by the stone you toss into a pond. Every business decision, every production or consumption choice, is a tossed stone that produces a ripple effect across the societal pond. You might want to take another perspective on this image by imagining yourself on a hill or in a tree overlooking the pond, but you have to remember that in matters of social responsibility, your choices make you a participant, never a mere observer.

CHAPTER TEN

The Common Good

Pursuit of the Common Good is a basic principle of ethical behavior; it is a bedrock principle like the principle of human dignity. Without it, social chaos would prevail. Yet, of all the principles around which I have organized this book, this principle is the most difficult for men and women in business to grasp and articulate. In fact, I have found that people generally, not just men and women in business, have difficulty in wrapping their minds (and hearts) around the notion of the common good.

Grady Means has an impressive resumé. He built and managed the PriceWaterhouseCoopers corporate strategy consulting practice after serving in the White House as special assistant to Vice President Nelson Rockefeller. He told me[1] that ethics, as framed in the principles presented in this book, is "a relative economic and legal issue, not a moral issue." The principles are relative in the sense that some of them work in some systems; some do not. "To discuss business ethics in the U.S.," he said, you have to "begin with acceptance of market systems and associated laws and practices."

He does not see individualism as an ethical issue; hence, a commitment to the common good as an antidote to individualism is unnecessary. The political system and the markets "define" fairness for him. "Independent definitions and opinions on 'ethics' and 'fairness' outside the market and political context are generally narrow and irrelevant," said Means. He added, "If you do not buy the view that markets are an efficient way to set prices and distribute goods and/or you do not buy that laws and policies define a society's opinion on fairness and ethics, then you are launching into a massive amount of opinion at odds with the collective decisions of hundreds of millions of your fellow citizens. That is what makes so many sermons or treatises on 'ethics' so problematic." He then framed for me what he considers to be the significant corporate "ethical" question: Does the company obey the laws?

It will come as no surprise to learn that Means believes that all the talk today about a crisis in corporate ethics is "nonsense and overblown rhetoric." Why, then, is everybody talking about it?

> As with many things, it is a manifestation of public scrutiny and mass media. Corporate behavior was far more problematic in the corporate monopoly and trust era a hundred years ago and the union-busting period fifty years ago. Fifty years ago, Andersen would still be in business, Ken Lay would be in his jet, and Martha Stewart would be in the Hamptons. Public scrutiny and the rules for ethical corporate behavior are vastly more complete and adhered to now than ever before.

Whether or not you find consistency and cogency in his arguments, I offer the views of Means, a friend whom I admire and respect, as evidence that the common good is not foremost on the minds of many thoughtful observers of contemporary corporate life. He thinks that "the principal objective for ethical corporate leadership is to manage the company for long-term growth in profitability, while conforming to all relevant laws and regulations." I would counter that corporate leadership should bear in mind its responsibility to contribute to the development and maintenance of a good and fair society, doing what it can for the benefit of everyone—or to say the same thing negatively, doing nothing that will harm anyone.

TENSION BETWEEN INDIVIDUAL RIGHTS
AND THE COMMON GOOD

On Sunday, October 3, 1992, Cardinal Joseph Bernardin of Chicago delivered the homily for the "Red Mass," celebrated annually in Washington, DC, on the Sunday prior to the first Monday in October, the traditional opening of a new term for the Supreme Court of the United States. Cardinal Bernardin's topic was, "Promoting the Common Good Through the Practice of the Virtues." The following excerpt speaks to the tension between individual rights and the common good:

> When considering the common good, it is far too easy to fall into the trap of seeing the common good as somehow opposed to individual rights and freedoms. This is a false dichotomy since individual concerns are inherently contained in any consideration of the common good. The common good is not concerned with the good of the community in a way that sets itself in opposition to the rights and freedoms of individual persons. In fact, the common good of the community is harmed when individual rights and freedoms are not respected. On the other hand, the individual is harmed when narrow self-interests and the pursuit of purely private gain are pursued without reference to the needs and interests of the community as a whole.[2]

Because profit seeking and profit making will always be factored into any serious conversation about the role of business in promoting and protecting the common good, this is as good a place as any to "read into the record" the words of Robert Wahlstedt, with whom I appeared on a panel discussing social responsibilities of business at St. Thomas University in St. Paul, Minnesota, about a decade ago. Wahlstedt, chairman and CEO of Reell Precision Manufacturing Company in Minneapolis, said:

We do not define profits as the purpose of the company, but we do recognize that reasonable profitability is necessary to continue in business and to reach our full potential. We see profits in much the same way that you could view food in your personal life. You probably do not define food or eating as the purpose of your life, but recognize that it is essential to maintain your health and strength so you can realize your real purpose.

When I bring that quotation to the attention of business school students, I usually add that they are unlikely ever, once they leave the fast-food world of college life, to hear any serious person advise them to maximize their intake of food!

Clearly, the principle of the common good is a communitarian ethical principle. It should prompt a wide-screen outlook on business activity. As Douglas Lalmont pointed out at an academic conference:

With the history of Enron and other corporate scandals now a part of our dialogue on business ethics, we know that the blind pursuit of self-interest does not always result in the common good.... The principle of the common good is based on the assumption that the flourishing of the community also enhances the well-being of the individuals in that community. This assumption is the precise converse of the liberal assumption made first by Adam Smith.[3]

He is referring, of course, to classical liberalism—*laissez-faire* economics—in mentioning Adam Smith, who believed, in Lalmont's words, "that individual pursuit of self-interest would naturally lead to the greatest aggregate good for all in that society.... Nevertheless, the blind pursuit of self-interest in recent times by corporations and their exotically wealthy CEOs has led many to question the truth of the claim that self-interest inevitably leads to the good of all."[4]

In a 2005 conversation with one of my Jesuit friends, Fred Kammer provincial of the New Orleans Province, the question came up of how well Jesuit colleges and universities are doing in preparing young men and women to advance the common good. Kammer once ran Catholic Charities USA and is a lawyer deeply committed to the promotion and protection of the common good. "We need students and graduates with dreams today," he said, "because we are a nation that has become increasingly cynical—about political leaders, about government, about public service, about the common good, and—beneath it all—about our own ability to create a better world, nation, city or neighborhood." What he said impressed me. Grady Means, to the contrary, said that free markets and regulatory law will not suffice to advance the common good. I think what Fred Kammer said is applicable to business circles where we also need practical, not cynical, men and women who can dream of a role for business in promoting the common good. But first we have to figure out what that notion really means.

UNDERSTANDING THE COMMON GOOD

The "common good" is a catch-all phrase that describes an environment that is supportive of the development of human potential while safeguarding the community against individual excesses. It looks to the general good, to the good of the many over the interests of the one or very few. The notion of the common good is not to be confused with a utilitarian principle that would say that the "right" action is whatever produces more good than evil for most of the community, or, to put it another way, the greatest amount of happiness for the greatest number of persons. Under this norm, something inherently wrong and plainly damaging to the common good would be permissible if the decision went by majority rule. So, in a world of ethical reflection large enough to move from personal and individual concerns to group or organizational issues and on out to global concerns, it is a matter of no small importance to have an appreciation of the notion of the common good.

Everyone knows you cannot tell a book by its cover, but I have to admit that the title on the cover of a small paperback prompted me to purchase *The Collapse of the Common Good: How America's Lawsuit Culture Undermines Our Freedom.*[5] The author is Philip K. Howard, who gave this book an earlier outing under the title *The Lost Art of Drawing the Line.* The title of another of his books, *The Death of Common Sense*, suggests he is preoccupied with the possibility that America is losing its grip on something important. This prompts me to ask in the words of Alfred Lord Tennyson, "Ah! When will all men's good/ Be each man's rule, and universal Peace/ Lie like a shaft of light across the land?" Do not look for that to happen soon, Howard would reply. "Legal fear has become a defining feature of our culture," said Howard.[6] The fear of lawsuits filed to reinforce individual rights has all but neutralized serious concern about the common good. Our founders would have been surprised by this, he said, because, as Howard sees it, "any notion of a common purpose is pushed aside by obsession with personal entitlement."[7]

That is worth thinking about as decision makers in business consider corporate social responsibility and the relationship of the business organization to the surrounding community.

We are losing a sense of working together to achieve common goals and protect the common good. Behind that loss is a reluctance to identify and articulate deeply held values. If, for example, the principle of human dignity is understood, accepted as a value, internalized and permitted to function as a prompter of personal choice, the person thus prompted will defend human dignity wherever and whenever it is under assault. Look around the workplace and the larger community for assaults on human dignity. Try to get behind the unemployment statistics. Look at urban decay. Examine the drug culture and its economic underpinnings. Ask about the physical environment within which low-income children seek both education and recreation. How about the estimated 45 million who have no health insurance? How does any or all of this relate to the common good?

In its document on "The Church in the Modern World," the Second Vatican Council of the Roman Catholic Church (1962-1965) described the common good as "the sum total of social conditions which allow people, either as groups or as individuals, to reach their fulfillment more fully and more easily."[8]

Another way—less abstract and far less lofty—of picturing the common good is to imagine it as an automobile tire, either the belted radials or the old-fashioned inner-tube tires. If tire or tube viewed as a whole looks integral and strong but has a cut, leak, or other point of vulnerability at just one small point, the whole thing soon will collapse. Think of this as the "collapse of the common good!" One small, unattended point of weakness or vulnerability can lead to a collapse of the whole. If the wheel needs alignment, that one point of imbalance could run the whole thing off the rim (and the vehicle off the road). Patch the tube, plug the leak, repair the belt, balance the rim—or else it will all collapse. It is in the interest of the rich and powerful to assist the poor and powerless; they are all part of the same tire. It is in the interest of business to attend to the maintenance of the common good, to be socially responsible, to attend to the demands of corporate social responsibility, because any business firm is part of a larger whole.

REPAIRING AND RESTORING THE COMMON GOOD

The blind pursuit of individual rights threatens the common good. An effective but widely ignored social tool for meeting this threat is not only the principle of the common good, but the principle of participation as well. If everyone votes, volunteers, speaks up, reaches out, and, when necessity requires it, doubles up, shares, and conserves, the common good will be served, and the community will be preserved. It is time for business to apply its unique potential to the repair and restoration of the common good.

It is important, of course, that there be agreement in the community that the common good should always prevail over individual, personal interests. This recognition functions as a voluntary norm or guideline for regulating the potential for socially damaging consequences of any self-interested behavior. It also functions as a basis for laws that put limits on individuals. Although the common good is higher than any private interest, it will always respect the inviolable dignity of the individual human person. As I indicated earlier, it is difficult for business people, young or old, to fully appreciate the importance of the notion of the common good. One of my MBA students at Loyola College in Maryland put it this way: "The principle of the common good is aligned closely with social responsibility in that it requires us to be cognizant of the common good in our dealings and actions. However, the principles of the common good and social responsibility should not trump or supersede what I would call the 'principle of individual liberty.' "

Herein lies the irony. Individual liberty is indeed trumped at times when steps are taken to protect and promote the common good, and there are a lot of individuals who do not like it! To promote and protect the common good is the reason why governments exist. More on that in the next chapter where there will be a discussion of the principle of subsidiarity, the principle that has a way of keeping government in its proper place.

It is regrettable, I think, that the notion of the common good is so seldom invoked in public policy debates over issues like healthcare insurance, minimum wage, welfare reform, immigration, foreign aid. It is doubly regrettable that business is usually presumed to be on the negative side of these debates.

It is not often that workplace health, safety, civility, and compensation issues are discussed in terms both of the common good of the workplace community, as well as the good of the broader community of which the workplace is a part. In both the private and public sectors of policy making, the common good has to be factored into the decision-making process, if that process is to promote the good of all.

JOB SECURITY CONTRIBUTES
TO THE COMMON GOOD

In this new corporate culture of diminished loyalty and heightened insecurity, it is important to note that economic interests and the common good are both served by widespread job security. No one was ever made more productive by being made less secure. The contingent nature of employment contracts and the growing uncertainties associated with workplace life are eroding confidence and damaging the common good.

One of my MBA "fellows" (young professionals working on weekends for a degree) at Loyola, drew on past experience to tell me about a commendable practice in a place of previous employment.

> The company experienced peaks and valleys in demand that had a direct impact on production. We depended on sub-assemblies from sister facilities. When they were unable to make their shipments, we were unable to provide work to our associates. But we didn't want to lay people off whom we would be needing in times of peak demand. So we came up with what we called the "LOW" program—"Lack of Work." The name isn't all that imaginative, but it permitted people to volunteer to take time off, while retaining health benefits and a return-to-work guarantee when demand picked up.

This was done, she told me, with an eye to the common good. Moreover the company had a bonus program with payments based on actual annual base and overtime pay. The employees who were doing the company a favor by volunteering for LOW, were, of course, lowering their actual pay base for the calculation of any bonus that might be paid. "So we changed the definition of eligible earnings to that of scheduled (vs. actual) hours of work with actual overtime added in." This was an expression of appreciation to those whose voluntary participation in LOW served the common good of the company but meant fewer actual dollars in their overall pay.

What constitutes the common good in a particular set of circumstances and in a given historical context will always be debatable. But if there is no debate—if there is an absence of concern for or sensitivity to the common good in public discourse—then you have a clear indication that society stands in need of help. As a sense of community is eroding, concern for the common good declines. This is an obvious danger in an age of individualism. A proper communitarian concern is the antidote to unbridled individualism, which, like unrestrained selfishness in personal relations, can destroy balance, harmony, and peace within and between groups, neighborhoods, regions, and nations.

AN OBLIGATION TO CONTRIBUTE
AND A RIGHT TO PARTICIPATE

The New Dictionary of Catholic Social Thought contains an interesting article on the common good.[9] It makes the point that recent teaching presents two complementary themes relative to this concept, namely, the *obligation* of the individual to contribute to the common good, and the *right* of the individual to participate in the benefits of society.

Anyone who takes a moment to reflect on the fact that approximately 45 million Americans participate in no health insurance program today will be forgiven for expressing outrage at this obvious assault on the principle of the common good. The obligation "to contribute" has financial implications for all of us, but not all are willing to face up to them. The right "to participate in the benefits" that a society can offer applies, of course, to the uninsured. Big business, automakers in particular along with employers in general, is concerned about the business expense of employment-based (hence employer-provided) health insurance, the predominant form of health insurance in the United States. During the period of wage and price controls in the United States in World War II, employers offered a health benefit in lieu of wage increases. That benefit found its way into collective bargaining agreements. Today, employers want to reduce or eliminate the benefit. Those who retain it are looking for ways to have present employees pay a larger share, and past employees lose their claim to the benefit altogether.

This is a problem that will not go away; and because healthcare accounts for about 15 percent of our gross domestic product, the economic implications of how we handle this one dimension of the application of the principle of the common good are enormous.

Only recently have I met and become friendly with Morton Mintz, now retired from a distinguished career as a reporter for the *Washington Post*. He is still quite active, however, as a writer and lecturer. Mintz is puzzled over resistance in the business community to publicly financed universal health insurance. "During the 1990s," he told a Long Island audience in April of 2005, "I found myself increasingly struck that corporations that would do anything for a buck would do nothing for the buck that would easily be theirs were the current system of private healthcare insurance based on employment to be replaced by publicly financed but privately run healthcare for all."[10] His lecture was based on an article he had published earlier in *The Nation* under the title, "Single-Payer: Good for Business."[11]

Mintz argues that publicly financed but privately run universal healthcare, including free choice of physicians on the part of patients, "would cost employers far less in taxes than their costs for insurance. Universal coverage could also work magic in less obvious ways. For example, employers would no longer have to pay for medical care under workers' compensation." He also believes that this is something that the tax-paying public would generally support. Why then does the business community have no enthusiasm for it? The opposition is, among other things, emotional and ideological, says Mintz, who spoke about this with Raymond Werntz, who for many years ran healthcare programs for Whitman Corporation, a Chicago-based multinational holding company. Werntz told Mintz that a single-payer solution to the healthcare financing crisis should appeal to Americans because it would be Medicare for everybody, and Medicare is a popular program that business endorses and draws few complaints from its millions of beneficiaries. (If Medicare-for-everybody became a reality in the United States, those who could afford it would still be free to enhance their coverage by buying private supplemental insurance, so no one would be required to have less to guarantee minimum or basic coverage for all.) So where is the problem? CEOs of large corporations see it as something "that smacks of socialism," Werntz said, and therefore as "heresy." (Readers might recall the discussion in Chapter 9 of the ideological blocks to meaningful discussion of the notion of corporate social responsibility.)

The cost to the nation's private sector employers who are now providing health benefits, is, on average, about $3,000 per employee, and employers are chafing under the burden. America's big-three automakers operate in Canada as well as the United States. They know that Canada's single-payer system reduces their labor costs, relative to what they pay labor in the United States, significantly. But neither Ford nor General Motors, only Daimler-Chrysler, supports any proposal to introduce publicly financed healthcare insurance in this country.

"No matter how urgently needed," writes Mintz in his *Nation* article, "no matter how common-sensical, no matter how much bottom lines would be fattened, single-payer or other fundamental healthcare reforms stall unless backed by the business organizations that govern the government. The Clinton Administration learned this to its sorrow after proposing its complex, comprehensive plan." Mintz and other observers agree that business organizations effectively killed the bill. Opposition from private insurers was not surprising. Those not close to the lobbying scene (where issues affecting the common good are always subject to special-interest influence) may not have expected such formidable opposition from businesses like fast-food chains. They hire a lot of young people, often work them less than full time, pay them little, and rarely provide them with health insurance. You have to wonder why they would oppose a federal program that, at no expense to them, would make life better for their employees. Ideology has to be part of the explanation, as is "clubbiness" with powerful big business executives and a reluctance to break away from the pack by speaking up for the uninsured. Where is their concern for the common good?

Mintz and those he has been talking to about this problem think that access to affordable, high-quality healthcare should be regarded as a "public good," like highways, fire protection, and police, all of which get paid for by the public purse. One of his allies in the drive to convince business that single-payer is in the cost-saving self-interest of corporations is Deborah Richter, a Vermont physician. She believes that making this "a practical issue works. Trying to win support for it by making it a moral issue never works." I find that sad; Mintz finds it puzzling: "By resisting the merger of practicality with morality that universal healthcare embodies, Corporate America is blowing a supreme opportunity, to do well by doing good. Enlightened self-interest this is not."

DOING WELL BY DOING GOOD

Merlin Olson, the retired Deloitte & Touche partner, used the same words in spelling out his understanding of the common good. "The enlightened business enterprise," he wrote in a letter to me, "seeks to DO WELL (succeed in business) by

DOING GOOD (promoting the 'common good')." That's exactly how he wrote it. He then appended this short commentary: "I win—we win—when everybody wins." Not everyone would see it that way, however, because individualism does not always yield ground gracefully.

For better or worse, all of us in the human community are in the same boat. All of us have to work to keep it afloat and pull our respective oars if progress is to be achieved. Growth-minded, tax-resistant business decision makers who believe that "a rising tide lifts all boats" are challenged now to partner with the public sector in making sure the healthcare boat remains in the fleet. This challenges business creativity to be of service to the common good.

Reason, not just religion, stands behind this assertion of the Second Vatican Council's Constitution on "The Church in the Modern World": "[T]he obligations of justice and love are fulfilled only if each person, contributing to the common good, according to his [or her] own abilities and the needs of others, also promotes and assists the public and private institutions dedicated to bettering the conditions of human life."[12] We have examined justice in Chapter 5; the ethical principle of love will be the theme of Chapter 12. Spread out between justice and love is the notion of the common good, which without justice and love is simply unattainable.

Regis University in Denver, Colorado, houses an Institute on the Common Good. It describes its purpose as providing a "forum for the discussion of significant social issues among knowledgeable people representing diverse perspectives." Wisely, the Institute favors conversation over argument, because there are no winners or losers at the end of a thoughtful conversation, just better-informed participants. The Institute brings people together to listen and speak to one another "with mutual respect in the hope that understanding might replace mistrust and consensus might be reached to serve the common good." This suggests the importance of other principles under consideration in this book, if the common good is to be served. Without participation, there will be no conversation.

Without respect for another's human dignity, there will not be much listening. Without wide participation and attentive listening, no consensus will be formed, and without consensus, the common good will not be served.

Should room be made in all of this for the principle of patience? Without it, the common good will remain a desirable but elusive reality.

———————

The image I like to use in communicating an appreciation of the principle of the common good is that of an automobile tire. If the tire is flat, you are looking at the collapse of the common good. When the tire is firm, round, properly inflated, and perfectly balanced on the rim of a wheel, you see that every segment of the tire is a participant, so to speak, in the good of the whole. A moment's reflection will serve to remind that if any one point of vulnerability, any weak segment of the tire "springs a leak," the whole tire deflates; the whole tire suffers the consequence of any puncture or any failure to attend to that point of vulnerability. Solidarity is another word that helps describe the common good. "We're all in this thing together," is one way of describing in ordinary speech the reality under consideration here.

CHAPTER ELEVEN

Delegation (Subsidiarity)

Those who say the care of economic casualties and the creation of jobs should be "left to government," risk violating the principle of subsidiarity, which would allow neither decisions nor actions at a higher level of organization that could be taken just as effectively and efficiently at a lower level. This principle, more readily understood, perhaps, in terms of delegation, would push decision making down to lower levels, but there are times, most would agree, when government must act in the interest of the common good. And there will be instances when only government can address an issue properly and effectively.

In the present situation of persistent poverty, widespread layoffs, rising executive compensation, and income stagnation for those who are, so to speak, caught in the middle, new public policy initiatives are being proposed and enacted. Reflective thinkers, with no ideological prejudices against using tax policy for social purposes, are debating the wisdom of a measure that restricts cash compensation that a firm can expense (i.e., count as a cost of doing business) to $1 million or less. They can pay more, if they want to, but the extra would be taxable corporate income before it became personal (and again taxable) income to the executive. This has encouraged the use of stock options and other forms of non-cash compensation. Would it have been better (and more transparent) to let the corporations decide the appropriate cash level? Who should decide in any case—the government or private corporate decision makers?

Robert B. Reich, while Secretary of Labor in the Clinton Administration, made a policy proposal on February 6, 1996 that caught the attention of many who were still reeling from AT&T's announcement a few weeks earlier that it would lay off 40,000 employees over the next three years. Secretary Reich said in a speech given at the George Washington University School of Business and Public Management:

> If we want companies to do things which do not necessarily improve the returns to shareholders but which are beneficial for the economy and society as a whole—actions such as upgrading the general skills of employees, providing them with decent pension and health care protections, sharing more of the profits with them, and, when laying them off, retraining them and placing them in new jobs—we have to give business an economic reason to do so. One possibility would be to reduce or eliminate corporate income taxes only for companies that achieve certain minimum requirements along these dimensions.[1]

Discussion of alternate tax policies is always going to open up debate about the appropriate role of government in trying to remedy societal problems. Subsidiarity is a principle of social justice designed to keep government in its proper place.

THE PROPER ROLE OF GOVERNMENT

Respecting fully the principle of subsidiarity, there are many things that government can do in the face of economic dislocation. The extent to which government should do some of the following depends on the ethical extent of a given employer's obligation to assist those laid off, and indeed of the whole private sector's social responsibility to address this problem privately. In any case, here are a few things government can do: Enlarge the unemployment insurance system beyond income maintenance during layoff to a re-employment system designed to help people get necessary training and find new jobs. Existing federally financed job-training programs could be enlarged to include vouchers distributed to unemployed or underemployed persons who could purchase some education and skill training with those vouchers. Both pensions and health insurance should be portable and thus not only support people between jobs, but free them to search, take an occasional risk, and to move from job to job as opportunities arise. Some universal form of health insurance, mentioned in the last chapter, would be a desirable safety net for those who now lose their health benefits when they lose their jobs.

There are times when government, big government, must act, and there are times when government should stand aside and leave the solution of problems to private initiative. There are also times within both governmental and nongovernmental organizations that decisions should not be taken at the top when they can be handled more effectively and efficiently at lower levels of the organization. This is the whole point of the principle of subsidiarity. I find a useful image to explain this notion (and to generate a measure of commitment to it) in five bronze figures that are part of the seven-acre open-air memorial to Franklin Delano Roosevelt near the Tidal Basin in Washington, DC.

The principle of subsidiarity states simply, as I just indicated, that no decisions or action should be taken at a higher level of organization (government being the primary reference point here) that can be taken as effectively and efficiently at a lower level of organization. FDR was first elected to the presidency in 1932, in the depths of the Great Depression. Something simply had to be done about massive poverty and unemployment in this nation. Could the private sector do it? Or was the job so big that only government—the federal government—had to act? Roosevelt decided that only the government was up to the challenge, so he led a vigorous program of federal initiatives.

The five bronze figures of dejected men, with overcoat collars turned up and hat brims pulled down, are lined up against a wall awaiting the opening of a soup-kitchen door in the second "room" of the FDR Memorial, which represents the second term of the Roosevelt presidency. The "New Deal" was underway. A federal "Social Security" program had been enacted to address the monumental challenge of doing something to meet the needs of "one third of a nation" that the moving Roosevelt Second Inaugural rhetoric—inscribed on the wall of this section of the FDR Memorial—described as "ill-housed, ill-clad, ill-nourished." The task was too large for the private sector; only the federal government had the resources for effective and efficient action.

Every spring thousands of school children visit Washington to see the federal buildings, monuments, and memorials. Platoons of youngsters descend on the FDR Memorial; invariably the kids slot themselves in between the bronze figures and have souvenir snapshots taken. Unaided, they are quite unlikely to realize that the bronze figures represent their grandfathers or great-grandfathers. These children of prosperity, with their long life expectancy, good health, educational advantages and so much more, have to be helped to understand that something happened in the 1930s. Their visit to Washington can be a "teaching moment" to learn something about the principle of subsidiarity and its relationship to significant social problems. Sometimes government simply has to act. In this case had not government—big government— taken bold action, life would have been a whole lot different for those children who might otherwise have "missed the bus," so to speak, and a whole lot more in their childhood development.

A SMART WAY TO RUN A COMPANY

The principle under discussion here (and more easily grasped, I think, if we call it "delegation") should also apply in private-sector organizations, in ordinary workplaces. However, based on his experience as director of the Small Business Counseling Center at the Community College of Baltimore County,

Laurence Aaronson reminded me that this principle is "tough to impart" in the setting of a family business, "especially when delegation of key decision making would be to someone outside the family."

With that caveat in mind, think of subsidiarity or delegation as relating to the principle of participation and, ultimately, reducible to the principle of human dignity. That is how it works at Long & Foster, the nation's largest privately held real estate brokerage firm based in Washington, DC. Speaking of how CEO Wes Foster delegates to his top managers, company president Brenda Shipplett told the *Washington Post* when her boss was inducted into the Washington area's Business Hall of Fame, "We're used to doing a good bit on our own. That's a very smart way to run a company, to empower people so they have confidence in themselves."

Individuals are not to be ground under by impersonal, anonymous decision makers at higher levels in the organization. It is here that the word "delegation" serves to convey more clearly the meaning of the reality of subsidiarity. It is here that I shall turn again to Charles Rossotti, whose views on the importance of relationships were discussed in Chapter 8. From my interview with him as well as from *Many Unhappy Returns*, his book on his years at IRS, I want to report his views on how delegation worked to restore trust and improve both morale and efficiency at the IRS.

Reflecting on how his managerial experience in the private sector influenced his management style at IRS, Rossotti told me:

> There is a lot about management and leadership that is applicable to both sectors. It take a little while to learn the vocabulary, the lingo, and what was motivating people in government, where there is far more emphasis on process than results. Process is important in business, too, of course, but the degree to which it controls the ways things work there is less than it is in government. Government runs by rules and procedures. When I recruited people in

from the private sector, this was one of the first things I had to sit down and tell them. You can get things done, I'd say, but you can't override the rules and regulations. For recruitment, contracting, hiring—you've got to go through the process. A lot of people in government get so bound up in process that it becomes an end in itself. There's good reason for process, of course; you're dealing with the public's money. You have a public trust and that's a constraint on management.

MOVE AROUND AND LISTEN

Commissioner Rossotti made it a point to move around the country meeting with and listening to IRS managers. He wanted their views on the problems they saw in the system, throughout the organization. He heard many complaints "but one theme came through clearly—the IRS national office was strangling them with directives. If they could just be left to operate more independently, they could solve a lot of these problems on their own. . . . Lack of trust magnified every problem."[2]

Convinced that building on the good relationships and rebuilding the ones that were broken was "the key to regaining trust throughout the organization," the new commissioner went to work.

> As a critical first step, I could personally work on building relationships with a circle of people who were most important to the functioning of the IRS. Over time, we could expand this circle by setting up the IRS so that more and more of IRS management built more and more direct, trusting relationships with people inside and outside the agency. Over time, we could replace the abstraction of management with meaningful relationships of one person to another.[3]

It took a lot of travel and many meetings, but eventually Rossotti was able to reduce the volume of directives and simplify the rules for managers. He had four ground rules for the decision-making process designed to produce procedures that would show more respect for autonomy and delegate responsibility down and out from the national headquarters to the field offices: (1) no special-interest representatives; (2) share information widely; (3) strict limits on scope ("we wouldn't want to make any more decisions than were absolutely necessary to design and implement the new organization"); (4) fact-based, open decision process.[4]

And where did it all lead? Conditioned by his private-sector experience, and hoping to bury the old saying, "We've got what it takes to take what you've got," Rossotti's aim was to organize the IRS "around the needs of our customers, the taxpayers. Just as many large financial institutions have different divisions that serve retail customers, small to medium business customers, and large multinational business customers, the taxpayer base falls rather naturally into similar groups. Therefore, it is logical to organize the IRS into units charged with end-to-end responsibility for serving a particular group of taxpayers with similar needs."[5]

He explained not the specifics but the general product, as opposed to the process, in October 2000 to an audience of several hundred tax lawyers, tax accountants, and other IRS stakeholders with whom he and many IRS managers had worked to plan the reorganizations:

> Major changes to the IRS are taking place to improve dramatically the way we do business with you across the board. Yet you will also hear that in spite of this massive reorganization, nothing has changed. The phone numbers have not changed, and the revenue agent handling your case will be the same. IRS offices don't change. Where's the change? Here's the answer. The new organizational structure merely enables us to put into place the leadership teams I introduced, and the tens of thousands of IRS employees they will lead. It enables us to give them the authority, tools, and responsibility to make a differ-

ence. Over time, they—not the structure—will produce the real change in the IRS—the visible, tangible changes in service, compliance, and productivity—that you and taxpayers across the nation so much deserve and will finally see.[6]

The reorganization produced four "customer-based" operating divisions—(1) wage and investment income, (2) small business and self-employed, (3) large and midsize business, and (4) tax-exempt and government entities. Three functional units were in place to handle appeals, taxpayer advocate services, and criminal investigation. Two shared-service units, one for information systems and the other for facilities and procurement, serve the organization's operating needs—all under a national office staff of 1,000 and a chief counsel's operation with 2,600 employees.

Because it tends to be more results oriented, Rossotti told me, business did not hone his reconciling skills as well as government service did. "You learn things like that in government, and you can carry those skills back with you into the private sector."

Joe Torre, manager of the New York Yankees, may never have heard of subsidiarity and probably does not think much in terms of delegation. But he understands this basic principle well and expressed it in words anyone can understand when he remarked in a television interview that "Successful managers allow their players to play the game. And that's what I try to do." He would, however, have no serious disagreement with Myer Alperin, the Scranton clothing manufacturer, who says, "Delegate, but review; don't get blind-sided."

TRICKY AND SCARY

Merlin Olson cited for me "a management theory that actually works" in the following words: "The best decisions are made at the lowest possible levels, by those who are most affected and most involved in implementing the decisions."

But, he warns, "delegation is tricky and scary." Why? Because, he explains, "managers can and should delegate responsibility. When they do, they must delegate authority. But they cannot delegate accountability for subordinate failure. It's impossible to pass the buck downward."

"Delegate and hold accountable for results" is one of fifteen principles that J. Willard Marriott used to build a successful business. All these principles were passed down as guidelines to run the company in a letter from father to son when J. W. Marriott, Jr., became executive vice president in 1964.[7] Here are some of the other principles on that list:

> People are No. 1—their development, loyalty, interest, team spirit. Develop managers in every area. This is your prime responsibility.
>
> Men grow by making decisions and assuming responsibility for them. So be sure to (a) make crystal clear what decision each manager is responsible for and what decisions you reserve for yourself; and (b) have all the facts and counsel necessary, then decide and stick to it.
>
> With respect to details: (a) let your staff take care of them, (b) save your energy for planning, thinking, working with department heads, promoting new ideas, and (c) don't do anything someone else can do for you.

There was a lot of practical wisdom embodied in the experience of the elder Marriott who advised his son to "manage your time" in the following three ways: "(1) keep your conversations short and to the point; (2) make every minute on the job count; and (3) work fewer hours—some of us waste half our time."

A Marriott executive, not a member of the family, told me that his personal assimilation of these principles convinced him to: "Let others lead. Share the praise. Let those with knowledge decide. Always surround yourself with people smarter than you. Hire great people and get out of their way."

Norman Augustine, former chairman and CEO of Martin

Marietta, likes to quote Yogi Berra's remark, "You can see a lot by observing." Augustine's observations are published in a management book called *Augustine's Laws.*[8] There are 52 of them, all famous for their humor—for example, the "Law of Perpetual Emotion" states, "Two-thirds of the Earth's surface is covered with water. The other third is covered with auditors from headquarters." The author gets serious in an epilogue that has this to say about the topic of the present chapter: "Delegation, wherever practicable, is the best course. Centralize goal setting, policy formulation, and resource allocation and decentralize execution. Managers at all levels need the latitude to do their jobs. As Plato suggested, justice is everyone doing his own job."[9]

Author and former publishing executive John Storey gave me his personal copy of *The Soul of the Firm,* by C. William Pollard, when he heard that I was working on this book. Pollard was chairman of ServiceMaster Industries, Inc., when he published his book in 1996. Storey liked Pollard's introductory observation that "what you are about to read is not just another 'business' book. While it contains principles of leadership, it is not just a book about how to lead. While it includes a discussion on the importance of profit, it is not just a book about how to make money. It is, rather, a book about people and their work. It is about the firm as an organization of people at work. It is about people at work who make up the soul of the firm."[10] In a book written to meet these objectives, I was not surprised to find mention made of "subsidiarity" and clear application of this principle to the real world of business. *The Soul of the Firm* is studded with principles in bold-face print, serving as dividers within every chapter and, in combination, amounting to a compendium of Pollard's personal set of management principles. In a chapter titled "Empowerment Comes from Power," he writes:

> We must as leaders embrace the principle of subsidiarity. It is wrong to steal a person's right or ability to make a decision. If we do so, it will ultimately cripple the firm,

with people caught up in activities to please their boss rather than to satisfy the customer. Delegation and decision-making at the point close to the customer are imperative. Delegation without a framework of authority, however, will result in chaos.[11]

Pollard's book includes a letter offering advice to his successor as ServiceMaster CEO, Carlos Cantu. Here is a portion of Pollard's advice that relates to delegation:

Be a champion of subsidiarity and growth. How best to organize a firm to both empower and maintain direction will be a continuing challenge. How big should the branches be? How big should the company units be? We know from experience that growth and size are related. . . . We also know that there are economies of scale and efficiency of greater size. There is a tension between these two points and it needs to be managed. My expectation is that we keep a bias toward line versus staff, sales versus operations. Keep pushing down decisions. Err on the side of delegation and not centralized control. In my judgment, centralized control will inevitably create a bureaucracy that will stifle the organization.[12]

A CAUTIONARY NOTE

In a book that describes, among many other things, "lessons learned" from his service as CEO of IBM, Lou Gerstner has an important reflection on subsidiarity. "For much of my business career, it has been dogma that small is beautiful and big is bad. The prevailing wisdom has been that small companies are fast, entrepreneurial, responsive, and effective. Large companies are slow, bureaucratic, unresponsive, and ineffective. This is pure nonsense."[13] He goes on to lay out the conventional wisdom:

Decentralization had a powerful intellectual underpinning, and over the course of a few decades, it became the "theory of the case" in almost every industrial and financial enterprise. The theory was very simple: "Move decision making closer to the customer to serve that customer better. Give decentralized managers control over everything they do so they can make decisions more quickly. Centralization is bad because it inevitably leads to slower decision making and second-guessing of the people on the firing line, closest to the customer. Big companies are inevitably slow and cumbersome; small companies are quick and responsive. Therefore break big companies into the smallest pieces possible[14]

Acknowledging that "there's a lot to be said about the power of this construct," and that it should influence organizational behavior in large corporations, Gerstner's doubts prompted him first to make a prescient comment about the danger of a decentralized U.S. intelligence community[15] and then to point out how strategic integration, rather than wholesale decentralization, spelled salvation for IBM. It is not, he argues, a question of centralization versus decentralization; it is a question of balancing "common shared activities with highly localized, unique activities." You share activities where you find natural and reasonable economies of scale—data processing, purchasing, real estate management, to mention just a few. With respect to the marketplace and customers, look for common systems and linkages between and among various parts of the business. Here, of course, some profit-center managers are going to have to yield ground. After making the point that decentralization can go too far, Gerstner says, "I quickly add that there is a ditch on both sides of the road. My concern is that today many CEOs are seeking utopian levels of integration."[16]

With some measure of confidence, a company can plan on taking advantage of economies of scale by integrating "back of the office" functions. Similarly some "front of the office" functions like customer databases and customer-relations management systems can yield integrated information, available to all divisions, about all customers. Not easy, but doable. However, the third and most difficult, as Gerstner sees it, area of common activities involves a "shared approach to winning a marketplace, usually a new or redefined marketplace. These activities are difficult because they almost always demand that profit-center managers subjugate their own objectives for the greater good of the enterprise. As such, they can be enormously controversial inside a company and lead to bitter and protracted struggles."[17] Generally speaking, he would advise CEOs against getting into this third level of integration unless they really have to. "Category three is very much a betthe-company proposition."

Why the pessimism?

One of the most surprising (and depressing) things I have learned about large organizations is the extent to which individual parts of an enterprise behave in an unsupportive and competitive way toward other parts of the organization. It is not isolated or aberrant behavior. It exists everywhere—in companies, universities, and certainly in governments. Individuals and departments (agencies, faculties, whatever they are called) jealously protect their prerogatives, their autonomy, and their turf. Consequently, if a leader wants fundamentally to shift the focus of an institution, he or she must take power away from the existing "barons" and bestow it publicly on the new barons. Admonishments of "play together, children" sometimes work on the playground; they never work in a large enterprise.[18]

This is the voice of executive experience speaking.

Gerstner did nonetheless take the step into area three, which is why he called his book, *Who Says Elephants Can't Dance?* Big companies can outmaneuver small companies. IBM saved itself by pulling off an "historic turnaround" (as the book's subtitle claims) that transformed the company from an organization that sold computers and software into, as business writer Allan Sloan put it, "a company that solved problems for customers by integrating computer systems."[19] The leap out of mainframes into services saved the company and it was, says Gerstner, "the most difficult and risky change" he ever made.

The IBM story tempers, but by no means negates, the principle of delegation. It serves the useful purpose of suggesting how important some of the other principles are—think, for example, of participation, the common good, and love, the principle that will be discussed in the next chapter—to shaping the environment within which any given principle can work. Each principle is important; all are essential to keep the business system on the tracks and moving in the right direction.

———

A simple ladder can serve as a useful image to catch the spirit of subsidiarity and the meaning of delegation. People understand those "up and down the ladder" comments that are often made with regard to corporate hierarchy. Many will remember the "Up the Down Staircase" movie title, even if they forget the point of the movie. Everyone has seen kids try to run "up the down escalator" in department stores and public places. Whatever works—ladder, escalator, elevator—to suggest that there are lower levels that might be more appropriate for a particular decision than the absolute top level will be useful.

CHAPTER TWELVE

Love

One reason why the old ethical principles have continuing relevance in this new corporate culture is the fact that they are rooted in a human nature that does not change all that much from age to age. Underlying human nature in any circumstance is the law of love. I list the law of love as the tenth and last of the "old" ethical principles. The challenge today is not to find a replacement for the law of love, which is always applicable, of course, to God, self, family, neighbor, and workplace associates; the challenge is just to let love happen in this new but still very human corporate culture. Anyone intent on releasing the potential of love in the workplace can make a significant contribution to the transformation of the world of work. The attitudes of freedom, openness, and vulnerability that characterize what may appear to be an idealistic ethical scenario are just what is needed to release that potential.

Take, for example, Paul Tillich's definition of love, "the drive toward the unity of the separated,"[1] and apply it to the typically divided workplace. Closing the gaps, healing the rifts, bringing it "all together" for the good of the organization is a labor of love. Tillich gives his notion of love a bit more play with the interesting observation that it cannot be described "as the union of the strange but the reunion of the estranged."[2] Clearly, love belongs in the workplace, dependent, as it is for efficiency and effectiveness, on teamwork and some semblance of a unified purpose. Getting the "estranged" together is the manager's job—again, a labor of love.

Just as love is congenial, natural, and familiar to anyone in possession of a human nature, opposing forces are also not unfamiliar to all of us ordinary mortals. We have to deal with pride, avarice (sometimes called "covetousness" and not all that different from "greed"), anger, envy, sloth (also known as laziness), gluttony (typically focused on food, but not all that different from "greed"), and lust (which can express itself in pursuit of sexual pleasure, material possessions, or power over others). These negatives leave little room for love; all of them are strangers to humility; and these negatives, as you may have been prompted to recall, are often listed as the seven capital sins.

The point here is simply to name the negative tendencies and to begin getting comfortable with the offsetting idea of love as a practical workplace reality. Put another way, the challenge is to remove from the workplace any vestiges of Budd Schulberg's "On the Waterfront" philosophy—"You do it to him before he does it to you"—and substitute Rabbi Abraham Joshua Heschel's conviction that "Our problem today is not to figure out how to worship in the catacombs, but how to remain human in the skyscrapers."

LOVE-DRIVEN LEADERSHIP

At the end of a seveteen-year career in investment banking with J.P. Morgan, Chris Lowney, who at an earlier stage of his life spent five years as a Jesuit seminarian, wrote a book that applies principles of Jesuit or Ignatian (the name derives from Ignatius of Loyola, founder of the Jesuit Order) spirituality to the world of business. The book is called *Heroic Leadership: Best Practices from a 450-Year-Old Company That Changed the World*.[3] Lowney finds in Ignatian spirituality "four unique values that created leadership substance: self-awareness, ingenuity, love, and heroism."[4] Business, says this business veteran, needs "love-driven leadership." By that he means a business leader should have "the vision to (1) see each person's talent, potential, and dignity; (2) the courage, passion, and commitment to unlock that potential; and

(3) the resulting loyalty and mutual support that energize and unite teams."[5] An emphasis on the development of others in a workplace is a signal that love is present. Love displaces fear. "Those who would rather help peers succeed than watch them fail are creating environments of greater love than fear. . . . Those who treat others with respect and love are leading the way to environments of greater love than fear, where many more people will enjoy the chance to achieve their full human potential."[6]

In a mother-to-daughter letter offering advice to her child on preparation for leadership, Anita Borek, a nursing supervisor at Johns Hopkins University Medical Center, explained to me that she told her daughter:

> When you lead, you will need to serve those around you instead of being served. You will need to coach them and remove obstacles that get in their way. Having been used to being a "doer" of the tasks, you will have to adjust to letting others get hands on. Since you enjoy doing things, this may be tough for you. When your competence at doing things opens up the door to leading people, you should recall the times that your superiors put you first. This is a kind of love in the workplace—when we let others do what we have loved doing. Remember that you were first given a chance; now give that chance away again. It does take time to show others how to do what you already do efficiently, but take that time. Then others will know that you love them and that is what leadership is really all about.

Song writers celebrate the special power of love to "make the world go 'round." Wisdom suggests that love is also needed to turn around the world of business. It is awkward, however, to talk about love in the context of business. It should not be, but it is. It is helpful, therefore, to notice how other words are employed, and have been for centuries, to convey the meaning of love. "Caring" is one such word. Consider this excerpt from "The Way of Life" by the Chinese sage Lao Tsu who, in the sixth century BC, wrote:

> When a man cares, he is unafraid.
> When he is fair, he leaves enough for others.
> When he is humble, he can grow.
> Whereas if, like men of today, he is bold without
>   caring,
> Self-indulgent without sharing,
> Self-important without shame,
> He is dead.
> The invincible shield of caring
> Is a weapon from the sky
> Against being dead.

What if that had been on every wall throughout the executive suites of Enron and WorldCom? It is not difficult to imagine the enhancement of any workplace where genuine caring is part of the atmosphere. Self-indulgence and self-importance yield to consideration for others and for their genuine growth. Caring is a thoroughly human characteristic. It serves to keep self-interest within appropriate boundaries; it is an expression of love. And if the "He is dead" assertion, describing anyone who is "bold without caring," comes as a shock to the modern reader, it should not. John the Evangelist makes the same assertion in early Christian literature (1 John 3:14): "We know that we have passed from death to life because we love our brothers. Whoever does not love remains in death."

Steve Dymowski, the MBNA vice president who regularly consults with others to make sure he is being fair, has a practical workplace understanding of love-as-sacrifice. He explains it this way: "At work, I often find myself sacrificing my time to ensure that people I work with are achieving their potential. As the people I lead earn promotions, allowing them to achieve their personal goals more effectively, I get a personal return on my sacrifice and gain a fuller realization of the responsibilities of leadership."

This bears out the finding of James M. Citrin, whom *Fortune* magazine calls a "high profile headhunter" with the Spenser Stuart search firm; he has placed CEOs in a broad range of companies including Yahoo and Eastman Kodak. In reporting on Citrin's book, *The 5 Patterns of Extraordinary Careers* (Random House, 2003), *Fortune* interviewed the author and asked a question that is relevant here: "You say the people who do best also help others. Isn't that counterintuitive?" The author's reply:

> Our research shows that 90 percent of the people defined by our criteria as extraordinary, focus on the success of those around them as much or more than on their own success. Average employees to an overwhelming degree focus on their own success. There are highly visible exceptions to this rule, but if you make those around you successful, you'll be successful by definition. It might take a little longer.[7]

Most of those who do this probably never think of it as a practical manifestation of love.

SPEAKING FROM EXPERIENCE

Michael Connelly, CEO of Cincinnati-based Catholic Healthcare Partners, acknowledges the sacrifice-dimension of love, but he points out that an effective way to bring love into the workplace is simply by having and showing "a passion for the work." Carroll Suggs will make the same point in her advice to up-and-coming managers in the last chapter of this book.

Jack Conroy, chairman of Investment Properties Corporation in Naples, Florida, is an independent director of Federated Funds. Another Federated director referred me to Jack who, at the time of this study, was on a sabbatical from his primary vocational responsibility to pursue an avocation—

graduate study in theology at the University of Notre Dame!
Not surprisingly, he had something to say on the principle of
love.

Conroy agreed to participate in my inquiry by writing out
in some detail his reflections on each of the ten principles.
(His advice to his own children, as well as to young associates
in his business, are included in Chapter 13). He says that love
"is a principle that has its roots only within a religious context, and cannot be grounded except within a religious framework." He continues: "Reflective Christians will see this principle as the ultimate expression of virtue, and the lynchpin of
a virtuous person." Prompted by his experience in business,
not his theological studies, he adds: "The difficulty of promoting this Christian virtue is that there are so many counterfeit 'Christian' values out in the workplace, that it immediately creates suspicion. Whenever a person tells me what a
good Christian person she or he is, I make sure my wallet is
still in my back pocket!"

Business ethics, in Conroy's view, tend to "relate to a set of
rules." That is a problem not only because rules tend to mul-
tiply, but because preoccupation with rules can miss the point
that virtue "is not a rule-book application." He goes back to
the Greek idea of "becoming good by being good," that is,
you make the right decision, not by following rules, but by
having a good character that is "inscribed on the person."

> The Greek word *charasso* means to "cut furrows, in-
> scribe." The noun that relates to that is "character," or
> that which is inscribed within the person. The method of
> inscription is traditionally considered "education." And
> today, "character education" is something being dis-
> cussed in schools. The problem has been that since Plato,
> the mere presentation of truth does not create an "in-
> scription" within the person. There is a prior step, seldom
> described, which is based on the old Celtic spirituality
> model, *anam cara*. Each person needs a model who has

incorporated the elements considered "virtuous," and who will encourage and assist other persons in the development of those behaviors that are affirmed by the model.

Jack Conroy is saying that the person of good character can model good behavior, ethical behavior, if you will, in the workplace. At the heart of good character is the virtue of love. Picking up on the Celtic theme, the one you love is an *anam cara*, "a soul friend," someone for whom you care. It is possible to bring the unseen reality we call love to expression in the everyday visibility of workplace care and consideration. "The root problem is that models are hard to come by, and principles are not necessarily well thought out," says Conroy. "Nevertheless, there is a starting point: The assumption that must be granted is that 'a virtuous life is the most happy life.' "

Vices are opposed to virtues. "The person who is not virtuous," says Conroy, "will become a vicious person," and he offers as an example "corporate officers who get away with looting their companies and having all the 'goodies' of our culture," without, however, enjoying a genuinely happy life— hence, the practical importance of bringing love to the workplace.

DO NOT WORRY ABOUT DEFINING IT

After reflecting over and responding to my questionnaire that covers the "old ethical principles," Ken Sparks, of the Federal City Council in Washington, DC, found himself thinking that it is "remarkable how the Golden Rule can serve as such a useful guide in practical business matters." Whether you think of it as a directive to "do unto others what you would have them do unto you," or simply, to "love your neighbor as you love yourself," the notion of love is there and, in Sparks's mind, it is accompanied by the idea of humility. An arrogant person is hardly a loving person. When you think how often "arrogance" is mentioned by commentators on Enron and World-Com, you have to wonder what life would have been like in those organizations had the principle of love been given more breathing room. Humility would have provided the opening love needed to influence for the better those warped business cultures.

I tend to associate humility in organizational life with the wisdom of Robert Greenleaf who encrypted the notion, so to speak, in the title of his famous book I mentioned back in Chapter 2—*Servant Leadership.*[8] Greenleaf, who died in 1990, was an executive at AT&T, thus fully familiar with the realities of corporate life. His view of love (he calls it an "undefinable" term) in a business setting is interesting. He sees its manifestations as "both subtle and infinite," but love begins, in his view, with "unlimited liability! As soon as one's liability for another is qualified to any degree, love is diminished by that much."[9] This view surely de-romanticizes the notion of love in a business setting, but it does not dismiss it. He points out that the British display practical wisdom in not applying "Inc." to corporations, but they openly acknowledge their "Ltd." or "limited" status. Our needs for goods and services are met in the marketplace by limited liability organizations; this does not suggest the absence of love, just limits. The stronger the sense of community in an organization, the higher the likelihood of love making its presence felt, but limits will always be there.

Peter Norris, president and group publisher for HMP Communications, has a very interesting take on the applicability of the principle of love in the workplace. He begins at home with the family (wife and two children), where love most appropriately and naturally belongs, and he consciously makes it visible in the workplace. He thinks "the greatest truth in humanity" is "wanting good things more for others than you want them for yourself." He has found that "living a loving family life" gives him "tremendous confidence" and enables him to communicate that confidence "to my workplace family." How does he do that? "By speaking highly of Jeannine (his wife) and adorning my office with pictures of the children." The result? "Everyone knows I value what I love; everyone sees how love builds confidence."

He is a practical-minded executive in a highly competitive medical magazine publishing business. Nonetheless, watching a video of "The Velveteen Rabbit" with his young children, Norris can connect the dots between a children's story and the reality of his own workplace. In the story, the Velveteen Rabbit asks the Skin Horse, "Will I become real?" The Skin Horse replies: "Real isn't how you are made. It's a thing that happens to you. When a child loves you for a long, long time, not just to play with, but really loves you, then you become real." If love, in the sense of caring, considerate, concern for others becomes an operative principle of workplace behavior, the workplace itself becomes more real and the relationships more genuine.

Nancy Itteilag is a star real estate broker with Long & Foster in Washington, DC. Her mentor, Wes Foster, is, according to the *Washington Post*, "a likable leader," "a formidable competitor" and "the consummate nice guy" to his top agents. "He works hard at keeping his agents happy, using his own brand of grandfatherly love," says the *Post*.[10] For her part, Itteilag responds to that love not simply by generating lots of business, but, as she told me, coming really to love her job. "If you *enjoy* what you do, applying the principle of love in the workplace is easy; if you don't you should find another job!" For many, love will manifest itself at work in terms of job satisfaction; and, thus satisfied, they find themselves becoming more fully human on the job.

LISTENING, LEARNING, SERVING

In Chapter 11 of this book, you read some of Bill Pollard's views on subsidiarity in a business setting. He is an executive firmly and personally committed to Robert Greenleaf's notion of servant leadership. He also has something to say about embedding the principle of love in the ordinary workplace.

Pollard mentions toward the end of his book *The Soul of the Firm,* an ascending order of ethical commitment—from Socrates' "know thyself," to Aristotle's "control thyself," to Jesus' "give thyself" ethic symbolized by the washing of the disciples' feet as recorded in the Gospel of John (13:1-15). Leaders, says Pollard, should "listen and learn." They should "work at making themselves available." They should "always be willing to do whatever they ask of others."

> At our headquarters building in Downers Grove [Illinois], we have designed our executive offices as a reminder of this principle of listening, learning, and serving. Nobody works behind closed doors. Glass is everywhere, confirming our desire to have an open office and open minds. No executive office captures an outside window. The view to the outside is available to all working in the office.[11]

I was intrigued to find explicit mention in this section of Pollard's book of those three qualities I have cited earlier from Dennis Goulet as essential for effective leadership. You will recall they are availability, accountability, and vulnerability, and you might see them now as expressions of love. Pollard insists that leaders should be "available" (p. 131); they should "provide an open environment in which their decisions and actions can be examined," so that they "cannot hide from the consequences of their decisions" (p. 132); and the good leader is "so open that sometimes he makes himself vulnerable . . .; it is this vulnerability that has brought power to his leadership" (p. 132). There is a lot in those few words to think about; they say something profound about the nature of love as they stake their claim for a place in the world of work.

"Servant leaders are givers, not takers," says Pollard; they "have their jobs because they can live without them."[12]

Brendan Green's review of Alban McCoy's book *An Intelligent Person's Guide to Christian Ethics,*[13] says "the tantalizing challenge at the end of this short book remains the problem of applying the law of love. If this attractive and creative approach to ethical judgment does not lead to a practical application that is also attractive and creative, then it might end up being dismissed as an unworkable pipe dream."

The writings of management theorists like Peter Drucker and Robert Greenleaf along with the practical experience of managers like Bill Pollard tell us that there is something attainable and practical (as well as "attractive and creative") in the application of the law of love. It is surely not an "unworkable pipe dream." That, by the way, is the expression— pipe dream—that Robert Bryce chose for the title of his interesting book about Enron, an organization not well known for the application of the law of love. In *Pipe Dreams: Greed, Ego, and the Death of Enron*,[14] Bryce says flatly that the company "failed because key leaders at Enron lost their moral/ethical direction at the same time that the company was making multibillion-dollar bets on fatally flawed projects."[15]

The same was true, he says, "for the Enron board members, the hapless, hoodwinked Greek chorus of fat cats—many of whom had special 'consulting' deals with Enron—who stood idly by while Enron was ruined."[16]

To say that management and board "lost" their ethical moorings is to imply that moral and ethical principles were in place to begin with. I don't think so. Unprincipled people making unprincipled decisions are the reason Enron collapsed.

"Tough love" finds its way into the vocabulary of family relations, especially parent-child interaction. For instance, there is a set of full-page newspaper advertisements posted by the Partnership for a Drug-Free America under the theme: "Parents: The Anti-Drug." One of these that I saw in the *Wall Street Journal* on September 15, 2003, had "The Enforcer" written over a picture of an African-American mother with her ear-ringed son in the background. Beneath the picture, this text: "She Doesn't Love Being Tough. She's Tough Because She Loves."

This idea was given a prominent position within management literature when an article by two British business consultants, Robert Goffee and Gareth Jones, appeared in the *Harvard Business Review*, in September-October 2000. A question they had put to countless executives in the United Kingdom and the United States during the previous decade supplied the title they chose to put on the article: "Why Should Anyone Be Led by You?"[17] "Without fail," the authors say, "the response is a sudden, stunned hush. All you can hear are knees knocking."

One of the "four unexpected qualities" that their research discovered to be present in truly effective and "inspirational" business leaders is the ability to manage employees with "tough empathy." This means that inspirational leaders "empathize passionately—and realistically—with people, and they care intensely about the work employees do." The three other qualities are: (1) selective disclosure of the leader's own weaknesses—exposing some vulnerability and thus revealing their approachability and humanity; (2) heavy reliance on intuition; the ability "to collect and interpret soft data [that] helps them know just when and how to act"; (3) revealing their differences—they "capitalize on what's unique about themselves."[18]

You can make it to the top without these qualities, but once there, you will find that no one wants to follow you. You will not be what these authors call an "inspirational leader." You could find yourself in a situation like that of a child in the back seat of an automobile with a toy steering wheel in hand. There is no connection to the wheels that carry the vehicle toward its goal. In any case, love is part of the inspirational leader's management tool kit. Goffee and Jones call it "tough empathy" to set it clearly apart from counterfeit concern for others. "Real leaders don't need a training program to convince their employees that they care. Real leaders empathize fiercely with the people they lead. They also care intensely about the work their employees do." This is clearly an application of the principle of love. It makes workplace love real, not theoretical; it has practical value for employer, employee, and their shared workplace. "Tough empathy means giving people what they need, not what they want. . . ."

> One final point about tough empathy: those more apt to use it are people who really care about something. And when people care deeply about something—anything—they're more likely to show their true selves. They will not only communicate authenticity, which is the precondition for leadership, but they will show that they are doing more than just playing a role. People do not commit to executives who merely live up to the obligations of their jobs. They want more. They want someone who cares passionately about the people and the work—just as they do.[19]

The "just as they do" tag is important. It serves to remind that this is not a one-way, top-to-bottom workplace dynamic. Empathetic love, whether tough or tender, should be pervasive in the workplace—up and down, across the board, throughout the organization. Those who gather there to work simply have to have the sensitivity to see its importance and the creativity to work it into their words and ways of doing things.

AN OPENING FOR FAILURE

We have discussed in earlier chapters the notion of "tone at the top" and the importance of first finding ethical principles "in the corner office" if there is to be any reasonable hope of finding them throughout the organization. There is no escaping the fact that not just the success, but the survival, of the CEO depends heavily on his or her ability to internalize these principles, not least the principle of love as explained in this chapter.

In the June 21, 1999, issue of *Fortune*, an article by Ram Charan and Geoffrey Colvin bears the title, "Why CEOs Fail." The reason, they say, is "rarely for lack of smarts or vision.

Most unsuccessful CEOs stumble because of one simple, fatal shortcoming." That fatal flaw, these writers say, is bad execution—that is, "not getting things done, being indecisive, not delivering on commitments."[20] Contributory factors are "failure to put the right people in the right jobs—and the related failure to fix people problems in time. Specifically, failed CEOs are often unable to deal with a few key subordinates whose sustained poor performance deeply harms the company."[21]

Many CEOs acknowledged to these authors that they knew there was a problem, but they suppressed the "inner voice" that was telling them do something about it. This failure, say Charan and Colvin, "is one of emotional strength." Translated into the language of this present chapter, the problem is typically a failure to understand the meaning of "tough empathy" and to apply the principle of tough love. The *Fortune* article says, "The best CEOs never hesitate to fire when they must, but the larger point is that they're deeply interested in people—far more so than failed CEOs are. . . . The motto of the successful CEO, worthy of inscription on his or her office wall, is 'People first, strategy second.' "[22]

You are not going to find much about love in the management section on the business shelves in your ordinary bookstore. This is not to say that love-driven leadership will not write "books" of its own in the human stories of workplace care and concern, as well as in the careers of those whose potential was released by the encouragement of workplace mentors. Love is happening in business now, and it can happen more. Its absence opened the door to corporate scandals; its presence will bar that door against the return of negative forces that will never be strong enough to overcome love.

The takeaway image I would offer for the principle of love in the workplace is the human smile—any smile. More often than not, when you see a smile, you see a sign of love. Your experience of life will remind you, of course, that love is often there in pain and suffering, and it is always there in true sac-

rifice. You may have encountered loveless smiles on occasion, but behind every genuine smile there is a spark of love. Moreover, most workplaces are populated with humans, and every human has the capacity not only to love, but to smile. The more the principle of love finds expression in the workplace, the more smiles will be there for all to see.

CHAPTER THIRTEEN

From One Generation to Another

This chapter provides a collection of recommendations given by experienced elders in response to my invitation for them to offer advice to a son or daughter, grandson or granddaughter, or to any newcomer who is open to some mentoring in the early stages of a business career. I often couched that request in the context of helping the young avoid the ethical quicksand that pulled down Enron, WorldCom, Arthur Andersen and so many others in the recent past. One manager I spoke to would recommend Robert Fulghum's book *All I Really Need to Know I Learned in Kindergarten* because, he said, "Wisdom is not at the top of the graduate school mountain, but there in the sand pile at school."

ADVICE FROM CYNTHIA DANAHER

I intend to let the veterans speak for themselves, and I will begin with Cynthia Danaher, retired general manager and vice president of Hewlett-Packard, who offers this advice to a young person she is mentoring.

Integrity enters the room before you; it stays after you leave. It is more important than any single thing you do. Do not ever compromise your integrity. If someone else tries to, stop them loudly and quickly.

Always be honest. Always look inside yourself and see your role in what happened. Be accountable for results. Never point blame, try to think about how you could have helped prevent the negative outcome.

If you are fair, people will relax in decision making. They will be kinder to others. They will respect the process and not feel they must end-run anyone else. They may not like what you decide, but they will respect it because you are fair.

Workforce reduction will often have to occur. Understand that each human being matters the same and must be treated with dignity. Too many companies equate salary level with value. Treat each person with dignity, the same as you would want to be treated. Even unpleasant tasks must be done with dignity.

Think inclusively. Every person wants to be a part of the discussion. Don't ever think your decisions are better; listen to others carefully. If you must make a decision alone, work to have others understand it. Put effort into inclusion; communicate with full facts. Your employees are very smart!

Care and follow through even when you no longer want to, even when it is difficult. Choose carefully the number of commitments you make. Choose a few things to be deeply committed to, and you will be more successful.

No action you take ends with you or your company. Always look around you. Always work to leave the community a better place than when you arrived. Social responsibility need not be sweeping in scope. Just contribute in any way you can but never be content not to contribute.

Understand the common good and communicate it to others. You may have to ask people to sacrifice for the common good. By showing or modeling this behavior, you will be pleased to find how much others are willing to do. But this is true only if the common good is understood and valued by the leader.

Hire people you trust and let them do their job. They may do things differently than you would, but let go. If you can't delegate properly, you have the wrong people in the jobs, or you may have to take a look at your control needs and how they impact others.

Give of yourself. Love can solve so many problems at so many levels. Do not be afraid of emotion. There is room for love in the workplace.

Finally, be wise. Do not lose your head in chaos. Think of the end. Always keep your eye looking to the distance, to the longer run.

ADVICE FROM TOM SAPORITO

Tom Saporito, senior vice president of RHR International, a consulting firm that specializes in corporate governance and organization, chose to write this letter to his son.

As you enter into a business career, you are embarking on an opportunity to put your talents to the test and also to make a difference in the lives of others. You are not, however, sitting down to a free lunch. You'll be facing decisions and choices that call for a thoughtful response. You'll need principles to help you navigate your behaviors and decisions.

Among your assets will be your desire to achieve and prove yourself worthy of responsibility, but you should know that these assets can cloud your choices. Make your frame of reference internal, not external. You have to know who you are and what you believe. This will be your baseline for negotiating the subtleties of decision making.

When you move into roles where you will be responsible for others—for example, giving feedback to others—organization dynamics might be such that it is far easier to avoid the important issues and side step telling the simple truth. There will be plenty of people and many organizational forces that will encourage you to hedge on what you should say or decide, and, indeed, there will be times when hedging is the way to go. But you have to ask yourself the question of what do you think the right thing to do is—what truly speaks to the dignity of others, not what is the most popular choice.

There will be endless challenges to your judgment of what is the right thing to do. The big issues tend to have obvious choice points. It will be the lesser issues that are laced with subtlety that will present the day-to-day challenges. This is where judgment comes in.

It will be tough to balance the needs of the organization

with those of the individual. That's when you have to look inside and reflect on your core values, and ask yourself the question: "What is the right thing to do here?" Then you can look others in the eye and feel confident that you are acting with fairness and integrity.

As long as you have a solid foundation of inner values and are sensitive to the needs of your different constituencies (your boss, shareholders, the "organization," subordinates, yourself) and use good judgment, you will be just fine!

You've been given a sacred trust to make a difference; use it wisely.

ADVICE FROM SISTER MARY KELLY: DEAR BRENDA

When I gave the keynote address to the Catholic Health Assembly (the annual meeting of the Catholic Hospital Association that attracts about 1,500 healthcare administrators), in Chicago in June 2004, I mentioned that I was working on this book and interested in knowing how any in that audience might advise aspiring hospital administrators with regard to organizational ethics. Sister Mary Kelly, R.S.M., chair of the health services administration department at the University of Detroit Mercy, took me up on the invitation and later sent me this "Dear Brenda" letter.

As you become a manager, I'd like to list a few things that I'd like you to remember. First, don't ever lie. Telling the truth is critical; otherwise, people will not trust you as a leader. Be who you say you are. Walk the talk.

You will have opportunities to play favorites. Don't do it, and you'll avoid all kinds of trouble (and time-consuming problems) by applying the same rules to all.

Be honest. If you can't share information, say so. Do not lie by silence.

Every person is just as good as you are; no one is any better. Believe this, and treat people accordingly.

Everyone has good ideas and insights. Use them. Invite and

structure ways for your employees to share in appropriate decision making. Limiting input is a great mistake; you'll miss a lot of opportunities if you do.

Choose a meaningful managerial role, and give your life to it. Hang in there!

Remember that you are always part of a community. You've been given much and must contribute to the rest of the community.

From a philosophical perspective, I endorse the notion of the common good and would direct your attention to the good of the whole community. However, from a very practical perspective, you should know that if you do not address "the common good," the bad effects will come back to you because "common" means just that—eventually you will experience the direct impact of what is missing elsewhere in society. You are always part of the whole.

When it comes to decision making, those closest to an area or issue will know the most about it. Ask them to help you make better decisions by telling you what they know and think.

Finally, each person is precious. You may not like them, but you must love them. Have at hand the virtues of mercy and compassion. Be a whole and loving person.

And with a practical wisdom that reflects a fair amount of time spent in the trenches, this veteran hospital administrator tells Brenda, "Culture can eat strategy for lunch. So be sure that the organization is what it says it is. Gently, but firmly, prune out of it any discordant behavior."

All organizational newcomers should be so fortunate as Brenda in getting this kind of mentoring advice!

ADVICE FROM GEORGE HOUSTON:
LESSONS FROM GEESE

George Houston, who was Georgetown University's chief financial officer for many years and whose introductory accounting course was famous there, spent the final nine years of a distinguished forty-three-year career in academic administration by serving as president of Mount Saint Mary's College in Emmitsburg, Maryland. He retained classroom contact with business students over the years and was an always available adviser to any who sought career direction. So it was natural for George to think of recent graduates when I asked him to offer advice to newcomers to business. He chose to use as a vehicle for his advice "Lessons from Geese," a set of maxims that he adopted personally and communicated to all of his associates in the academic workplace. There are five "lessons," each accompanied by a "fact." Houston first came across these in a management development seminar; to the best of my knowledge, they originated with Baltimore educator Dr. Robert McNeish in 1972. Here then, in fact-and-lesson format, are the "Lessons from Geese" that George Houston offers as guidelines for newcomers to business, and an outline for conversations with the young about getting off on the right foot as they step into business careers.

Fact #1: As each goose flaps its wings it creates an "uplift" for the birds that follow. By flying in a "V" formation, the whole flock adds 71 percent greater flying range than if each bird flew alone.
Lesson: People who share a common direction and sense of community can get where they are going quicker and easier because they are traveling on the thrust of one another.
Fact #2: When a goose falls out of formation, it suddenly feels the drag and resistance of flying alone. It quickly moves back into formation to take advantage of the lifting power of the bird immediately in front of it.
Lesson: If we have as much sense as a goose, we stay in formation with those headed where we want to go. We are willing to accept their help and give our help to others.
Fact #3: When the lead goose tires, it rotates back into the formation and another goose flies to the point position.
Lesson: It pays to take turns doing the hard tasks and sharing

leadership. As with geese, people are interdependent on each other's skills, capabilities, and unique arrangement of gifts, talents, or resources.

Fact #4: The geese flying in formation honk to encourage those up front to keep up their speed.

Lesson: We need to make sure our honking is encouraging. In groups where there is encouragement, the production is much greater. The power of encouragement (to stand by one's heart or core values and encourage the heart and core of others) is the quality of honking we seek.

Fact #5: When a goose gets sick, wounded, or shot down, two geese drop out of formation and follow it down to help and protect it. They stay with it until it dies or is able to fly again. Then, they launch out with another formation or catch up with the flock.

Lesson: If we have as much sense as geese, we will stand by each other in difficult times as well as when we are strong.

George Houston sums it all up in the following sequence of key phrases: *shared purpose* (which relates to what I've been calling "culture" in this book); *accept and give help* (sounds like "participation," as used in this book); *shared leadership* (this relates to what I've called "delegation" in these pages); *encourage others* (a form of "love"); and *stand by each other* (commitment).

ADVICE FROM CARROLL SUGGS: ONE CEO'S VIEW

Carroll W. Suggs, retired chairman and CEO of Petroleum Helicopters, Inc., chose to "look back" over her years of leadership in order to give me "One CEO's View" so that I could pass it on in this way to those in the early stages of their business careers. She begins by saying, "We are in a new game with new rules brought about by a number of major forces, including: (1) the globalization of business; (2) dramatic geopolitical shifts; (3) major socio-demographic changes that have a significant impact on workforce composition; and (4) rapid technological change." On an optimistic note, she remarks: "As a result of these forces, we have far more opportunities today than at any point in our history." And here is her advice to the young who are on their way up in business.

If you are in a leadership role, you will face challenges each and every day. The key for you and your organization is to learn and improve continuously. You must clearly articulate and communicate your values, your vision, and your strategy and involve and align your people with them. Your values and integrity are going to be tested in almost every aspect of your professional and personal lives.

The challenge with principles, you will find, is not in identifying them, but in having their practice become a habit. Your character will set you apart, as will your ability to understand people and your ability to work effectively with others.

To be great at something—to succeed—you must like what you do; indeed, you must truly love it. You will know in your heart whether or not you are passionate about what you are doing, and, just as importantly, so will others!

Some of my best learning and networking and most rewarding experiences are from volunteer work. I've been heavily involved in giving back to the community to improve the quality of education at all levels. Aside from education, some of the other organizations that I've long supported are Junior Achievement, United Way, Southern Eye Bank, Lighthouse for the Blind, the Foundation of the LSU Health Science Center, and the Louisiana Cancer Research Consortium. I always encouraged my employees to participate extensively in similar community activities wherever we operated throughout the world.

I envy the opportunities ahead of you. For me, it has always been the journey and not the destination that was fun, and challenging, and important.

I wish you all good luck and good fortune on your journey and great success in the realization of your dreams.

ADVICE FROM JACK CONROY:
LETTER TO MY CHILDREN

Jack Conroy, chairman and CEO of Investment Properties Corporation, used my ten principles as a point-by-point outline for a letter to his own children, as well as to young associates in his Naples, Florida, company. It will serve as a useful summary of the principles to follow this outline.

1. Integrity. No one wants to deal with someone who is two-faced. Be unpredictable, and you can forget about long-term business relationships. One has to decide, when beginning a business life, whether one wants to invest in the creation (and rapid destruction) of lots and lots of business relationships, or to deal with a relatively small number that remain alive for years and years. The former is inefficient but does not require integrity. The latter takes more time and more investment but is ultimately the most efficient way to be successful in business.

2. Veracity. It's going to happen soon into your career. You are going to make an error and will be forced to admit it. Short term, it might be appealing to attempt to avoid the acknowledgment of the error and to lie about it. But one never knows how it will come out; and the risk is that integrity, principle #1, yields to its opposite—being two-faced. The risk isn't worth it. This will happen when other bad news has to be communicated. In terms of risk and reward, recognize that sometimes the hardest way is the best way long term.

3. Fairness. The most difficult thing about fairness is that one must accurately understand what is owed to oneself in a transaction. Further, one's obligations to the client must be seen to be more important than one's own benefit from the relationship. Fairness means everyone's rights must be accurately assessed, and the outcome must be appropriate (proportionate) to those rights.

4. Dignity. There is a cultural bias that says, "Those people who are not just like me are somehow less valuable." This is

a bias that will produce disrupted relationships, and, consistent with the principle of establishing long-term relationships, it is risky to permit this bias to become operative. The bias can be countered by a heartfelt affirmation that every human being has an inherent dignity and is worthy of respect. This gets translated into being especially sensitive to insensitivity to gender, race, religion, and sexual orientation. Only a sense of integrity (note again the importance of principle #1!) can be relied upon here; if you harbor those biases, they WILL come out and will disrupt a relationship.

5. Workplace Participation. Make sure your superiors are aware that you want to be involved in decisions within your competence. And once you become a superior, remember how you felt about the importance of participation.

6. Commitment. This gets displayed every day in how you attack your job. It can't be faked. If it doesn't exit, it won't be perceived by others. And when promotion time comes, you will be overlooked. Once you advance in the organization, become a role model for others in terms of commitment to the right things, namely, those positive values that make any organization excellent.

7. Social Responsibility. From the earliest time of your career, be involved in making your community a better place. Initially, it might be as a Big Brother or Sister, or Scout leader. Belong to community, business-oriented organizations like Rotary or Kiwanis, that exist to assist the community. Later, when you are in a position of authority, don't forget the good things these organizations do. Involve your business in being a responsible corporate citizen.

8. Common Good. Recognize that we exist within a social framework where selfishness and greed create only a small number of apparent winners and lots of losers, and that such social structures have been crushed by history in terms of revolutions and social upheaval. A focus on the common good will produce benefits for yourself in the long term.

9. Delegation. Be willing to take chances early in your career. Be willing to make decisions and run the risk that you

might be wrong. Let your superiors know of your desire and then, when you advance in your organization, remember how it felt.

10. Love. Our Christian religious upbringing has sacrifice at its core. The Incarnation of Christ is not something that happened once in history and is subsequently forgotten except on Sunday mornings. The Incarnation made God visibly and tangibly present in our history. I like to think that this is our task, our obligation in business, indeed in everything we do—to make God present in our world. We, as believers committed to Christian values, make Christ present in our world by meeting our everyday business responsibilities. Some would call this "doing the right thing." That's fine, but I would also see it as a response to the invitation of our Brother, the Christ, to follow the pattern he laid out to help us lead the good life.

ADVICE FROM NANCY ITTEILAG

Nancy Itteilag, the real estate broker, used a hypothetical situation to impress upon her son, a summer intern with her firm, the importance of adhering to the Code of Ethics of the National Association of Realtors. She asked him to imagine that his best friend is trying to buy his first condo and that there are multiple offers on the same property. "Let's say that the property is listed in our office, and we've seen all the other offers before your best friend prepares his. You'll be tempted 'to help him out,' but you can't. How would it look if your best friend just happened to come in, after all the rest, with the best offer? Here's how you avoid any perception of wrongdoing or playing favorites."

1. Give your friend all the information from our computer on similar properties and how much people are willing to pay.

2. Encourage your friend to make the best offer he can afford, going in.

3. Let him know that if he loses (always a high probability), you'll continue to work with him. There will always be other properties coming on line.

4. You should present offers sequentially to the seller in the order in which they came in. Let the seller decide.

5. Have two agents present to ensure that all offers are presented fairly.

6. Once the seller decides, let all potential buyers or their agents know the result. Tell those who lost just how far off they were and, of course, tell them that you will call when a new opportunity for a similar property comes up.

That keeps it all fair and square, she said, before noting: "Above all, remember that it takes only one mistake to ruin a lifetime reputation, and no one deal is worth it, even if it's your best friend."

ADVICE FROM CHARLES WATSON

Nancy Itteilag's point about the fragility of a reputation built up over a lifetime is reinforced by Charles Watson's "icicle" image in this letter offering advice to his son embarking on a career in business.

Your word must always be your bond. Never give it unless you mean it and have reasonable expectations of being able to fulfill it. Honesty is like an icicle—once it melts it is gone forever.

So always be truthful; any lie is a capital sin. You don't always have to be blunt, and you can certainly avoid hurting others when you speak. Always find a way to tell the truth fully and in a timely manner. Withholding the truth is as wrong as lying. If there are lapses, face up to them promptly; covering up is a far worse failure.

When you find yourself in a position of authority, you'll realize that being fair to everyone is not easy. Think of fairness as a chess game in progress. Never make a hard decision without a lot of thought. It's okay to defer a decision until you've had sufficient time to think it through. Think about the possible choices—how they affect each piece on your chess board—not just now, but several moves down the road. With experience, hard decisions will come easier because you will have stored up some wisdom along the way. Over the years, I've found that the best solutions often come to me in the middle of the night!

Never consider yourself better than others in business. True class, by my definition, is being able to interact successfully with, and to understand, each person from the most important to the destitute. Every human being deserves respect; make sure you treat each one accordingly.

I think you should treat those with whom you work as a family. That means talking to others every day. Over-communicate, if necessary. If others don't know where the business is going and what it's going to take to get there, you can't blame them for not helping. Establish teams; realize that several brains are better than one. I'm convinced that "top management" is an oxymoron. Your organization will work best from the bottom up. If you can encourage your teammates to believe and take responsibility, they will admire you for it, and you'll find that the job is getting done. Don't take credit; always give it.

I hope you will locate your career in something that you really love doing. If you're not happy at work, you won't be happy at home. So think carefully before you commit yourself. Commitment means having faith in the principles that guide your company. If you don't believe in what your company produces, if you don't think its goods or services are the best—or that you can help make them become the best—don't take the job. You have to have a passion for not just meeting your customers' expectations, but for so far exceeding them that you generate delight all around.

You're going to find that the greatest rewards in business come from being truly engaged with the people and places you see every business day. If you want to be a good executive, an executive leader, then you're going to have to see unseen opportunities and put together the people and resources that can meet those opportunities. Think of a workplace community as a secular congregation, and think of anything you

can to improve that community as the highest form of enlightened self-interest. Get involved for the fun of it, and do
your best to make it fun for all.

Think of team management as a concept, a goal that you
can imagine, an image to be kept in mind. As an executive,
your most important job is being a great talent scout. Hire
the right people. Reward them well, and let them do the rest.
Make sure that you report to them as often as they report to
you.

Love your customers. Be kind to them. Be of real help to
them. Never allow them to sink into debt beyond their means.
Say no when you have to, explain why, and be prepared to
hear an occasional thank you for that no. Tough love in business, or any other area of life, is still love. All love involves
some sacrifice. You're going to find that your sacrifices will
return great joy along with truly rewarding lifetime relationships.

ADVICE FROM LAWRENCE CLARK

Lawrence Clark, who runs the employee assistance program at
the Middle Tennessee Medical Center, employed helpful imagery in a letter offering advice to his daughter Cam as she was
moving into a position as general manager. "Remember when
we used to go to the Jersey Shore?" he asked. "All those rivers
that eventually flowed into the bay and then the ocean had
those little poles stuck in the mud or sand to let boaters know
where the channel was clear and where the barriers were.

"Sometimes when a storm came, the markers had to be
repositioned, but always with the goal of keeping the boaters
safe—a very kind behavior for someone the boater might never
meet. The person who marked the channel for safety was doing
a very reverencing act. That's your responsibility now. Set the
markers clear to allow your people the choice to be safe. In
following the markers, they will be exercising their trust in
you. In setting the markers you will be exercising trustworthy
leadership."

ADVICE FROM PHILIP O'BRIEN

Philip O'Brien, a British businessman who spent 25 years with Honeywell and 10 with Mercury one2one, is Chairman of South East Excellence in London. He expressed interest in participating in this project when I met him at a conference in Oxford in October 2004. He decided to make some serious points in a whimsical way. He composed the following "Letter to a Nephew Eager to Make His Mark in Business" and appended to it a very creative set of suggestions. Both letter and the list of "Hints and Tips" are written in the satirical style of the famous *Screwtape Letters* of the English writer C.S. Lewis. This entertaining book is world famous for its portrayal of the human condition from the perspective of "Screwtape," a lieutenant of "Our Father Below," who, of course, is Satan. The worldly wise "Screwtape" dispenses advice to his nephew "Wormwood," who is just starting out on his own demonic career with an assignment to ensnare an innocent and unsuspecting young man. Lewis's classic is a humorous but also serious story of dealing with temptation. How clever of Philip O'Brien to notice its applicability and adaptability to the world of contemporary business.

Dear John:

Congratulations on your recent appointment in the world of big business. I'm sure you have a very bright and rewarding future ahead of you.

You seem to have an unerring eye for an opportunity—I heard about the business you set up at college, and your successful appeal against the expulsion campaign led by the Parent Teacher Association.

It was a good sign of your early awareness that other people's money can be diverted surprisingly easily—quite often even with their full co-operation—into your own bank account.

You may well be able to teach me a thing or two on the

finer points of today's ethics management, so I would welcome your comments on the hints and tips attached to this
letter.

Please keep in touch as your career progresses—I may be
able to help further downstream if only to stand bail. And
when you set up your own public company, I would certainly
want to hold some shares in it—for a while at least.

Yours in anticipation of future profits,
Uncle Philip

Enclosed: A Set of Useful Hints and Tips

Don't be misled into believing that integrity is important—
it's the appearance of integrity that counts. Groucho Marx
said, "The key to business success is integrity and honesty.
Fake that and you've got it made." Retain the flexibility of
being all things to all people—they rarely find you out in the
short term, and in the long term there is scope for apparent
humility and confessing to your human inconsistencies—for
which you might even attract the bonus of praise.

Veracity is an over-valued commodity. The truth is often
limiting and unprofitable. Sometimes it turns out to be incorrect anyway, so what's all the fuss about? Don't tell people
any more than you have to. Telling them what they already
know is often received very positively, boosting a warm glow
in the listener since you are confirming what they believe.
Also popular is telling people what they want to hear, even
when you know it's not true. You are simply jumping on the
same wagon as them, so it's more solidarity than lying.

Don't waste time and effort trying to be fair. Life is what
you make of it—the fact is there will always be winners and
losers. Often, if the losers weren't losing, there would be nothing for the winners to win. Just don't flaunt your winning in
the wrong places—it might make some losers suspicious and
reduce your chances of winning whatever they still have left.

Human dignity has a lot to be said for it, as long as what
you say doesn't have any effect on what you do. Be as re-

spectful as you can when face-to-face with those whose bank account is joining others as the supply chain into yours. It will postpone the day when they become aware of reality— by which time they are probably no longer of any value to you anyway.

I'm all in favour of workplace participation. These people are here because they need to be here—their participation should be at least 100%. Keep them overloaded so they feel needed but have to work at home in the evening or at weekends to hit their deadlines. In that way their family may even participate in your cost-reduction priorities for free.

Demand total commitment from your staff, and let them know by occasional staff-reductions that they can depend on your total and unswerving loyalty—to the bottom line.

The broader community can see you as a friend if you make a few low-cost gestures toward some touchy-feely project of no business relevance. Hold a "family day" at the factory and lay on balloons and ice cream. But make it a Sunday to avoid any loss of production. Donate leftovers to the children's nursery down the road, and get your photo in the local press. Then your application for planning permission will meet with fewer objections.

Talk frequently about the common good whenever there is contention about changes affecting the work force. There are always some who can gain from changes that put others at risk. Give them a good reason to join you in supporting your changes, thereby shifting the balance in your own favour. After all, when the losers have left or been let go, the good is common to those who remain.

Delegation, when used appropriately, can ensure a rapid rise through to higher management untroubled by the baggage of wrong or misguided decisions. Don't hesitate to delegate responsibility for unpopular actions to several people whilst giving the impression that each one is the chosen one— the crown prince perhaps. But avoid giving authority and resources along with responsibility. Keep them strictly under your own control. The ultimate delegation is, of course, to your successor as you move smoothly into a more senior position before the long-term negative effects of short-sighted decisions are fully visible.

Be generous with your time, attention, and resources. Lunch in the company restaurant and chat with people in the queue. Sign off dubious expense reports without question. Be friendly and approachable in the good times, so you won't feel guilty about not "loving thy neighbour" when it's a matter of saving your own skin at the expense of his.

Finally, understand the importance of self-sacrifice. Many a glittering career has foundered in the past on this hurdle. But today, a spell in jail can be the kicking-off point for a whole new career winning fresh markets. By choosing your misdemeanour carefully, you can move on to scale even greater heights from a start point elevated by a judicious investment in atonement.

A FINAL THOUGHT

These specimens, serious even when offered in a humorous mode, serve three purposes. They help to summarize the main lines of this book. They offer sound advice from experienced veterans who care enough for the next generation of business leaders to provide it. The presence of the elders, particularly the retired elders, in these pages serves to suggest that it would be a wise move for anyone under 40 in the world of business to put him- or herself in touch with a mentor. Once over 40, business executives would be well advised to cultivate friendships with younger members in their organizations (as well as outside)—occasional, informal contact, social, professional, business formal, or business casual—all for the purpose of staying in touch with younger minds, new ideas, fresh dreams. Similarly, those under 40 should be both humble and wise enough to realize that it is important for their future and the maintenance of their own humanity to be connected with the elderworld. Once connected, everybody wins!

Two 33-year-olds—one male, the other female—responded

to me, through one of the elders whose advice is offered in this chapter, by saying that when they were younger, distinguishing good from bad was easy. "We learned from Star Wars." But now, they say, they find themselves in "a world of contradictions."

> We say we care about a fair wage, but really we mean we want cheap clothes. We say we care about the environment, but we do not stop driving our pollutomobiles. We say we want to learn lessons from the past, but we do not respect our elders. (Let's face it; we would only listen to what you say about ethics if we happen to feel we are flailing with an ethical dilemma.)

"We think you are suggesting that ethics is something we have to learn to become conscious about," they continued. "In which case we believe ethics is as much about *reflection* as it is about action. Because how can we ever know the full impact of our decisions? Should we not find out whether *others* perceive us as being ethical? They might give us a different insight into when and how we are not adhering to ethical principles."

I would surely agree that a rise in ethical consciousness is what I am hoping this book will promote. I would also agree that attention to the perceptions of others is useful, but I would say to this reflective pair that what others think should never become normative for adherence to ethical principles. They see ethics "as a dynamic force that looks for harmony within a moral and philosophical system which is bigger than just ourselves. The more we consider ourselves in the context of the 'bigger picture,' the more we are required to step outside of our own frame of reference to act ethically." They have to wrestle, they say, with the problem that "moral and ethical actions that appear clear when aspects are viewed in isolation, become much murkier in a larger view frame."

Fair enough; nothing in these pages can be taken as a guarantee that it is going to be easy.

"If ethics is evolving," they ask, "should we spend some thought as to where we are going? What new windows of opportunity should we be looking through? Do we create our ethical future with a vision of how we want the world to be, or does ethics simply evolve naturally over time and human experience?" Whatever the nature of the evolution, I would hope that ethical principles not explored in this book, namely, principles of courage and competence, become part of ethical discourse.

I am convinced that the principled person with principled vision can find his or her way through the "murkiness" into a more ethical future. It is an impossible journey only for those whose destination is themselves. These two 33-year-olds hope to find "harmony within a moral and philosophical system which is bigger than just ourselves." That outlook suggests to me that they are already on the right track.

―――――――――

The takeaway image for this final chapter is the baton. Not the baton held in the hand of an orchestra leader, rather the baton handed on from one runner to the next in a relay race. One generation always "passes the baton" to the next. In this chapter older, wiser, more experienced managers have passed along wise advice to younger sprinters who, it is to be hoped, will become successful long-distance runners in their own generation of business leadership.

ACKNOWLEDGMENTS

I owe a debt of gratitude to many friends and lots of strangers for helping me bring this project to completion. Tom Donnelly provided financial assistance and warm encouragement right from the beginning. My agent Mike Snell, an expert on putting together book proposals, was a great help in bringing the project into focus. Joe Langmead, retired partner of KPMG, read the manuscript and helped me understand much of the accounting mischief hatched by Enron and Arthur Andersen that misled investors, eroded pension funds, swallowed over 20,000 jobs, and destroyed countless careers.

The names of many others are on the lines, between the lines, and behind the pages of this book. To give them all their due, I want to thank: Laurence Aaronson, Shep Abell, Myer Alperin, Dan Altobello, Dorsey Brown, Jim Burke, Lawrence Clark, John Cleveland, Michael Connelly, Jack Conroy, John Coughlan, Paul Coughlin, Cynthia Danaher, George Ferris, John Fontana, Dan Geer, Chuck Geschke, Lou Giraudo, Joe Giuliani, Bill Glavin, Fred Gluck, Hubert Gordon, Steve Harlan, Sam Hazo, Larry Herbster, Henry Hockeimer, Shel Horowitz, George Houston, Nancy Itteilag, Larry Johnson, Mary Kelly, Joe Kraemer, Ralph Lancaster, Barry LeBlanc, Jim Leeper, Sal Lenzo, John Levert, Chris Lowney, Jim Maguire, Chip Mason, Madeleine Mauwer, John McDaniel, Steve McEwen, Paul McNamara, Grady Means, Phil Merrill, Morton Mintz, Bill Morley, Paul Montrone, Morey Myers, John Nahas, Jeannine Quain Norris, Peter Norris, Philip O'Brien, Merlin Olson, Fiona Philip, Steve Potts, Robert Reed, Gerry Roche, Charles Rossotti, Tom Saporito, Iain Shearer, Bill Sondericker, Bonnie Soodick, Ken Sparks, Suzanne Stahl, John Storey, Carroll Suggs, Dom Tarantino,

John Thomas, Dick Thornburgh, Charles Watson, and Marion Wielgosz.

The Integrity Quotient in Chapter 3 is reprinted with permission of America Press.

Dean Lee Dahringer, of the Sellinger School of Business and Management at Loyola College in Maryland, provided me with the academic perch I needed to do the research, along with support and encouragement along the way.

My thanks to all. Or, as close readers of the text might expect me to say, "Much obliged!"

NOTES

INTRODUCTION

[1] "Sweeping Up the Street," *Business Week*, May 12, 2003, 114.

[2] See, for example, Archie B. Carroll and Ann K. Buchholtz, *Business & Society: Ethics and Stakeholder Management*, 4th ed. (Mason, OH: South-Western College Publishing, 2000), 44.

[3] Bethany McLean and Peter Elkind, *The Smartest Guys in the Room: The Amazing Rise and Scandalous Fall of Enron* (New York: Portfolio [Penguin Books], 2003).

[4] McLean and Elkind, xxi.

[5] "Capitalism and Democracy," *The Economist*, June 28, 2003, 13.

[6] "Capitalism and Democracy," 13.

1. OLD ETHICAL PRINCIPLES

[1] I like Bernard Lonergan's definition of culture: "A culture is a set of shared meanings and values informing a common way of life, and there are as many cultures as there are distinct sets of meanings and values." *Method in Theology* (New York: Herder and Herder, 1972), 301.

[2] Willa Cather's 1923 tribute to Nebraska was quoted in Henry Steele Commager, *The American Mind* (New Haven: Yale University Press, 1950), 154.

[3] See George C. Lodge, *The New American Ideology* (New York: New York University Press, 1986), 15-21.

[4] Jeffrey E. Garten, *The Mind of the C.E.O.* (New York: Basic Books, Perseus Publishing, 2002), 140.

[5] William Faulkner, speech given in Stockholm, December 10, 1950, upon receiving the Nobel Prize in Literature.

[6] Boeing, *Ethical Business Conduct Guidelines* (undated), 5.

[7] *Wall Street Journal*, March 8, 2005.

[8] Alan Murray, "Indiscreet E-Mail Claims a Fresh Casualty," *Wall Street Journal*, March 9, 2005.

⁹Geoffrey Nunberg, "Initiating Mission-Critical Jargon Reduction," *New York Times*, August 3, 2003.

¹⁰Roger Lowenstein, *Origins of the Crash: The Great Bubble and Its Undoing* (New York: Penguin, 2004), 42.

¹¹Ibid., 43.

¹²See "Q&A with Al Golin," *The Public Relations Strategist*, Fall 2003, 28-29.

¹³*Business Week*, March 29, 2004, 91.

¹⁴Francis Fukuyama, *Trust: The Social Virtues and the Creation of Prosperity* (New York: Free Press, 1995), 6-7.

¹⁵Lowenstein, *Origins of the Crash*, 226.

¹⁶This image suggestion came from a conversation I had with Larry Johnson, co-author with Bob Phillips of *Absolute Honesty: Building a Corporate Culture That Values Straight Talk and Rewards Integrity* (New York: Amacom, 2003).

2. THE NEW CORPORATE CULTURE

¹See Michael Eskew, "Delivering on the Promise" in *Building Trust: Leading CEOs Speak Out* (New York: Arthur W. Page Society, 2004), 254-269.

²Terrence E. Deal and Allan A. Kennedy, *The New Corporate Cultures* (New York: Perseus Publishing, 1999), 4.

³Ibid., 3.

⁴Charles Handy, "What's a Business For?" in *Harvard Business Review on Corporate Responsibility* (Cambridge, MA: Harvard Business School Press, 2003), 66.

⁵It is interesting to note that Lynn Sharp Paine chose *Value Shift* as the title for her 2003 book (published by McGraw Hill), which traces the development of a new and now widely accepted standard of corporate performance that adds moral considerations to the financial-only measures of the older corporate culture.

⁶Peter F. Drucker, *Managing in a Time of Great Change* (New York: Truman Talley Books/Plume, 1995), 17.

⁷Robert K. Greenleaf, *Servant Leadership: A Journey into the Nature of Legitimate Power and Greatness* (Mahwah, NJ: Paulist Press, 1977), 9-10; (emphasis in the original). This book is now available in paperback and should be part of every manager's personal library.

⁸John K. Waters, *John Chambers and the Cisco Way* (New York: John Wiley & Sons, Inc., 2002), 40-41.

⁹As reported in the *New York Times*, September 17, 2003.

[10]Editorial, *New York Times*, July 14, 2003.

[11]Steve Lohr, "The Ascent of the Software Civilization," *New York Times*, March 9, 2003.

[12]*Business Week*, October 8, 2001.

[13]Jack Valenti, speech given at Duke University, Durham, North Carolina, February 24, 2003.

[14]Stephen L. Carter, *Integrity* (New York: Harper Perennial, 1996), 29.

[15]Arthur Levitt, *Take on the Street* (New York: Pantheon Books, 2002), 19.

[16]Frank Taylor as quoted in Joseph L. Badaracco, Jr., *Leading Quietly: An Unorthodox Guide to Doing the Right Thing* (Cambridge, MA: Harvard Business School Press, 2002), 98.

[17]John Gardner, *Self Renewal* (New York: Harper Colophon Books, 1965), 124.

3. INTEGRITY

[1]John E. Flaherty, *Peter Drucker: Shaping the Managerial Mind* (San Francisco: Jossey-Bass, 1999), 269.

[2] James E. Burke, interview with author, February 20, 2004.

[3]Charles Watson, *Managing with Integrity: Insights from America's CEOs* (New York: Praeger, 1991).

[4]Ibid., 20.

[5]Stephen Carter, *Integrity* (New York: Harper Perennial, 1996), 7. Carter acknowledges influence in forming this understanding from Martin Benjamin's book *Splitting the Difference: Compromise and Integrity in Ethics and Politics* (Lawrence, KS: University Press of Kansas, 1990).

[6]Ibid., 47.

[7]Robert O'Connor quoted in Alec Klein, *Stealing Time: Steve Case, Jerry Levin, and the Collapse of AOL Time Warner* (New York: Simon & Schuster, 2003), 212.

[8]Woodstock Theological Center, "Creating and Maintaining an Ethical Corporate Culture" (Washington, DC: Georgetown University Press, 1990).

[9]Ibid., 7.

[10]Raymond J. Murphy, "Like Father, Like Son," *America*, vol. 107, no. 20 (August 18, 1962), 614-615.

[11]Arthur Miller, *All My Sons*, in *Three Plays about Business in America*, edited and with introductions by Joseph Mersand (New York: Washington Square Press, 1964), 184.

¹²Arthur Miller, *Death of a Salesman*, Act One (New York: Penguin Books, 1949), 56.

¹³Robert Bolt, *A Man for All Seasons* (New York: Vintage Books, 1960), 81.

¹⁴Fred Hassan, "Business Integrity," in *Building Trust: Leading CEOs Speak Out* (New York: Arthur H. Page Society, 2004), 29.

¹⁵Transcript provided by Federal News Service, Inc., Ste. 220, 1919 M St., NW, Washington, DC 20036.

4. VERACITY

¹"Kmart Accuses Former Officials of Misconduct," *New York Times*, January 25, 2003.

²Roger Lowenstein, *Origins of the Crash: The Great Bubble and Its Undoing* (New York: Penguin, 2004), 226.

³Sue Shellenbarger, "How and Why We Lie at the Office," *Wall Street Journal*, March 24, 2005.

⁴Sisela Bok, *Lying: Moral Choice in Public and Private Life* (New York: Vintage Books, 1999), 109, 249.

⁵Michael Jordan, "Putting the Client First," in *Building Trust: Leading CEOs Speak Out* (New York: Arthur W. Page Society, 2004), 174.

⁶Fred Weisman, speech, *CWRU/Magazine*, Summer 2003, 10.

⁷"UBS Analyst Is Forced Out for Health South Remark," *New York Times*, July 3, 2003.

⁸Floyd Norris, "A New Morality Makes Old Deceptions Expensive for Wall Street," *New York Times*, October 8, 2004.

⁹Don Aucoin, "Let's Be Honest," *Globe Sunday Magazine*, August 10, 2003.

¹⁰Robert C. Baumhart, S.J., "How Ethical Are Businessmen?" *Harvard Business Review*, vol. 39, no. 4 (1961), 26-31.

¹¹Margaret O'Brien Steinfels, "Can We Tell the Truth?" in *Resources: A Service of Boston College*, Spring 2003, 15.

¹²"Fuzzy Numbers," *Business Week,* October 4, 2004, 79-81, 128.

¹³Ibid., 79.

¹⁴Ibid.

¹⁵Ibid., 80-81.

¹⁶Ibid., 128.

¹⁷Arthur Levitt, *Take on the Street* (New York: Pantheon Books, 2002), 13-14.

¹⁸Bethany McLean and Peter Elkind, *The Smartest Guys in the*

Room: The Amazing Rise and Scandalous Fall of Enron (New York: Portfolio [Penguin Books], 2003), 39.
[19]Ibid.
[20]Ibid., 40.
[21]Ibid., 127.

5. FAIRNESS (JUSTICE)

[1]Barbara Ward (Lady Jackson), "Looking Back at *Populorum Progressio*," *Catholic Mind*, vol. 76, no. 1327 (November 1978), 9-25, note 1.
[2]See http:www.communitariannetwork.org. The survey "What do voters want? A fair society" was delivered electronically to the network on July 29, 2004.
[3]Samuel Hazo, "Scientia Non Est Virtus," in *Just Once: New and Previous Poems* (Pittsburgh: Autumn House Press, 2002), 29.

6. HUMAN DIGNITY

[1]Quoted by Walter J. Burghardt, S.J., in *Justice: A Global Adventure* (Maryknoll, NY: Orbis Books, 2004), 12. The reference is to Donahue's booklet "What Does the Lord Require? A Bibliographical Essay on the Bible and Social Justice," *Studies in the Spirituality of Jesuits*, vol 25, no. 2, March 1993, 8.
[2]Donahue, "What Does the Lord Require?" 12.
[3]Burghardt, *Justice*, 25-16.
[4]Alice McDermott, *Charming Billy* (New York: Dell, 1998), 91-92.

7. WORKPLACE PARTICIPATION

[1]Albert V. Casey, *Casey's Law: If Something Can Go Right, It Should* (New York: Arcade, 1997), 315-316.
[2]Bill George, *Authentic Leadership* (San Francisco: Jossey Bass, 2003).
[3]Ibid., 167.
[4]Richard L. Thornburgh, "Some Lessons to be Learned from the Breakdown of Corporate Governance at WorldCom," speech at a meeting of the Committee on Federal Regulation of Securities of the American Bar Association, December 5, 2003.
[5]Robert K. Greenleaf, *Servant Leadership* (Mahwah, NJ: Paulist Press, 1977), 63.
[6]Ibid., 94.

[7]Ibid., 117 (emphasis in the original).

[8]Paul Davis, "Outsourcing Can Make Sense but Proceed with Caution," *Chronicle of Higher Education,* January 28, 2005, B20-22.

[9]Ibid., B22.

[10]Charles O. Rossotti, *Many Unhappy Returns: One Man's Quest to Turn Around the Most Unpopular Organization in America* (Cambridge, MA: Harvard Business School Press, 2005).

[11]Ibid., 178.

[12]Ibid., 224.

[13]Ibid., 293-299.

[14]Ryuzaburo Kaku, "The Path of Kyosei," in *Harvard Business Review of Corporate Responsibility* (Cambridge, MA: Harvard Business School Press, 2003), 107.

[15]Ibid., 113.

8. COMMITMENT

[1]Joanne DeLavan Reichardt, "Corporate America's New Secret Weapon: Trust," *The Public Relations Strategist,* Fall 2003.

[2]John Gardner, *Self-Renewal: The Individual and the Innovative Society* (New York: HarperColophon, 1965), 118.

[3]Ibid.

[4]Lynn Sharp Paine, *Value Shift: Why Companies Must Merge Social and Financial Imperatives to Achieve Superior Performance* (New York: McGraw Hill, 2003), 177.

[5]Charles O. Rossotti, *Many Unhappy Returns: One Man's Quest to Turn Around the Most Unpopular Organization in America* (Cambridge, MA: Harvard Business School Press, 2005).

[6]Ibid., 83.

[7]Ibid., 87.

[8]Ibid., 88.

9. SOCIAL RESPONSIBILITY

[1]David Collins, "A Lesson in Social Responsibility," *Vermont Law Review,* 27 (2003), 825-831.

[2]Ibid., 827.

[3]Ibid.

[4]Johnson & Johnson, "Our Credo," available at http://www.jnj.com/our_company/.

[5]Steve Hilton and Giles Gibbons, *Good Business: Your World Needs You* (Mason, OH: Thomson, 2004), 69-70.

[6]Ibid., 95.

[7]Joel Bakan, *The Corporation: The Pathological Pursuit of Profit and Power* (New York: Free Press, 2004).

[8]Ibid., 2.

[9]Ibid., 57-58.

[10]Ibid., 62.

10. THE COMMON GOOD

[1]Interview with Grady Means, October 13, 2004.

[2]Joseph Bernardin, "Promoting the Common Good through the Practice of Virtues," *Congressional Record*, October 12, 1993, E2402.

[3]"The Common Good and the 'New Corporate Culture,'" paper delivered at a conference on Catholic Social Thought across the Curriculum, University of St. Thomas, St. Paul Minnesota, October 23-25, 2003, 2 and 4.

[4]Ibid., 4.

[5]Philip K. Howard, *The Collapse of the Common Good* (New York: Ballantine Books, 2001).

[6]Ibid., 11.

[7]Ibid., 122.

[8]"The Church in the Modern World" in *The Documents of Vatican II*, ed. Walter M. Abbott, S.J. (New York: America Press, 1966), 225.

[9]Judith A. Dwyer and Elizabeth L. Montgomery, eds., *The New Dictionary of Catholic Social Thought* (Wilmington, DE: Michael Glazier Books, 1994), 192-197.

[10]Morton Mintz, "Corporate America Will Do Anything for Big Bucks—Except Single-Payer," lecture delivered to the Long Island Coalition for a National Health Plan, Garden City Community Church, on April 5, 2005.

[11]Morton Mintz, "Single-Payer: Good for Business," *The Nation*, November 15, 2004.

[12]"The Church in the Modern World," 228.

11. DELEGATION (SUBSIDIARITY)

[1]Robert B. Reich, speech at George Washington University School of Business and Public Management, February 6, 1996.

[2]Charles O. Rossotti, *Many Unhappy Returns: One Man's Quest to Turn Around the Most Unpopular Organization in America*

(Cambridge, MA: Harvard Business School Press, 2005), 85.

[3]Ibid., 88.

[4]Ibid., 178-179.

[5]Ibid., 174.

[6]Ibid., 191.

[7]Full statement available from the Marriott Corporation, Employee Communications and Creative Services Department, Marriott International Headquarters, Marriott Drive, Washington, DC, 20058, 800-638-6707, x-1023.

[8]Norman R. Augustine, *Augustine's Laws* (New York: Viking, 1983).

[9]Ibid., 364.

[10]C. William Pollard, *The Soul of the Firm* (New York: HarperBusiness, 1996), 16.

[11]Ibid., 102.

[12]Ibid., 140.

[13]Louis V. Gerstner, Jr., *Who Says Elephants Can't Dance? Inside IBM's Historic Turnaround* (New York: HarperBusiness, 2002), 242.

[14]Ibid., 243.

[15]"The problem of decentralization exists in government, too. The United States intelligence community is a hopeless hodgepodge of overlapping yet ferociously independent organizations. When a new threat arises (such as domestic terrorism), the task of redirecting the intelligence assets of the country away from the missions they were originally designed to carry out to meet the new challenge becomes an integration task of gigantic proportions." Ibid., 243.

[16]Ibid., 246.

[17]Ibid., 246-247.

[18]Ibid., 249.

[19]Allan Sloan, "In 'Elephants,' Gerstner Holds an Unfocused Gaze," *The Washington Post*, November 19, 2002.

12. LOVE

[1]Paul Tillich, *Love, Power, and Justice* (New York: Oxford University Press, 1954), 25.

[2]Ibid.

[3]Chris Lowney, *Heroic Leadership: Best Practices from a 450-Year-Old Company That Changed the World* (Chicago: Loyola Press, 2003).

[4]Ibid., 9.

[5]Ibid., 170

[6]Ibid., 201.

[7]"Not Your Average Headhunter," *Fortune*, July 21, 2003, 40.

[8]Robert K. Greenleaf, *Servant Leadership* (Mahwah, NJ: Paulist Press, 1977).

[9]Ibid., 38.

[10]"A Likable Leader: High Regard for Agents, Strong Competitive Spirit, Keep Wes Foster on Top," *Washington Post*, November 20, 2004, F1.

[11]William Pollard, *The Soul of the Firm* (New York: Harper Business, 1996), 131.

[12]Ibid., 138.

[13]Brendan Green, "Review of *An Intelligent Person's Guide to Christian Ethics*," *The Tablet*, November 27, 2004, 21.

[14]Robert Bryce, *Pipe Dreams: Greed, Ego, and the Death of Enron* (New York: PublicAffairs, 2002).

[15]Ibid., xi.

[16]Ibid., xii.

[17]Robert Goffee and Gareth Jones, "Why Should Anyone Be Led by You?" *Harvard Business Review*, September-October 2000, 63-70.

[18]Ibid., 64.

[19]Ibid., 68.

[20]Ram Charan and Geoffrey Colvin, "Why CEOs Fail," *Fortune*, June 21, 1999, 70.

[21]Ibid.

[22]Ibid., 74.

INDEX

Also by William J. Bryon, S.J.

Toward Stewardship (1975)
The Causes of World Hunger (editor, 1982)
Quadrangle Considerations (1989)
Take Your Diploma and Run (1992)
Take Courage: Psalms of Support and Encouragement (editor, 1995)
Finding Work without Losing Heart (1995)
The 365 Days of Christmas (1996)
Answers from Within (1998)
Jesuit Saturdays (2000)
A Book of Quiet Prayer (2006)

ABOUT THE AUTHOR

William J. Byron, S.J., is research professor in the Sellinger School of Business and Management at Loyola College in Maryland, where he teaches corporate social responsibility in the MBA program.

A native of Pittsburgh, he received his early education in Philadelphia. After military service as an army paratrooper in 1945-1946, he enrolled at St. Joseph's University for three years of study before entering the Society of Jesus (Jesuit Order) in 1950. Fr. Byron was ordained to the priesthood in 1961. He holds degrees in philosophy and economics from St. Louis University, two theology degrees from Woodstock College, and a doctorate in economics from the University of Maryland. He is past president of the University of Scranton (1975-1982), The Catholic University of America (1982-1992), and served as interim president of Loyola University in New Orleans during the academic year 2003-2004.

Fr. Byron taught social responsibilities of business in the McDonough School of Business at Georgetown University from 1993 to 2000, and during that period served as rector of the Georgetown University Jesuit Community. From 2000 to 2003, he was pastor of Holy Trinity Catholic Church in Washington, DC.

His bi-weekly general interest column, "Looking Around," is syndicated by Catholic News Service, and in 2004 he began writing a monthly "What Do You Want to Know?" feature for *Catholic Digest*.